Musical CHAIRS

The Mystery

DRIFT WALKER

BALBOA
PRESS
A DIVISION OF HAY HOUSE

Balboa Press books may be ordered through booksellers or by contacting:

Balboa Press
A Division of Hay House
1663 Liberty Drive
Bloomington, IN 47403
www.balboapress.com
1 (877) 407-4847

Print information available on the last page.

ISBN: 978-1-5043-3822-6 (sc)
ISBN: 978-1-5043-3823-3 (e)

Library of Congress Control Number: 2015912615

Balboa Press rev. date: 08/19/2015

INTRODUCTION

The train made more noise than ever as it went by overhead! I found a place to yell and scream out the things I was upset about and all the wrongs done to me. The place was in between very large timbers that made a bridge for the train to go over a lake channel. I was feeling great after yelling and screaming all the bad things that happened to me. After the train passed, I was climbing down from the railroad bridge or 'trestle'. As I climbed out from inside the large timbers, I twisted my body to get out of the small opening. For a second, I let go of the timber with my left hand and tried to reach it with my right hand as I straightened up, but my right hand never touched the timber and I fell backwards, head first.

The timber I was on was about 10-15 feet off the ground.

I saw the rocks below and readied myself for impact! At first I was confused when a white veil of light surrounded me. Simultaneously, I was held in place by a force that was all comforting. I struggled right away, but almost as quickly, I was okay with being held in place. At first I could see through the veil of bright white light. I could see the water and the rocks, under the car bridge, the channel going into each bay and everything was getting more blurry. After I knew I was okay, the bright white light became blindingly bright. I could no longer see anything around me or in the background, only white.

I knew I was okay, I knew I was being held, I saw the blinding white light get brighter and brighter and then I could see only me in a scene, but the scene is real life, my life was playing in front of me!

The bright white light went away. It was replaced with better than three dimensional scenes of my life happening in front of me, one at a time. I could not change anything that happened to me, but I could move around in the scene anywhere I wanted to move too. Scene after scene played before my eyes all the way back to before my birth! It seemed to take the same amount of time to view as it did to live out each scene.

When my life was done playing before my eyes, the bright white light was present again and I was blinded by it again. I was now back in a crouched position ready to grab the timber and I did!

I grabbed it and held on for dear life. I held on to the timber long enough to realize that it was too long. I climbed up to a level place and started feeling my arms and legs to make sure I was okay and not hurt. I looked around to see if anyone was watching me. I was embarrassed at first! How was I going to explain to anyone watching that I was held in mid-air by a bright white light? That the bright white light showed me my whole life in more detail than any movie available.

Then I came to my senses after a minute or so of my confusion. I looked up to where I think heaven is and thanked Our Father for sharing my life with me. I promised him I would write it all down and share it with others like he shared it with me. I promised I would serve him.

Our Father is watching and recording everything we do.

I climbed up to the deck of the bridge and walked a block home. I remembered my real Dad! I remembered he let me drive his car when I was a little boy. He would let me stand up and turn the wheel and steer the car! Our Father shared memories of my real family with me! He saved me from scratches, cuts, a sure bump on the head or worse when I fell backwards. He placed me back up to a safe place again when he was done showing me everything. Wow did I feel good!

I knew I was in for trouble when I opened up the door to the Foster parent's house. I had no idea what time it was but I knew I was late. I didn't care though. For the first time in as long as I could remember, the bright white light was around me. Our Father was around me. I have a whole other family. By watching my life pass before my eyes, I remembered Drift and Eva were not my parents. I opened the door with something I was going to tell Drift.

I walked in the door at Drift and Eva's, they were eating dinner. Drift told me since I was late, I could go to my bedroom without dinner. I told him I remembered my real parents. I told him he was not my Dad and that Eva was not my mom and Drift hit me. Before I could say another word, Drift punched me in the face! I never had a plan of what to do when he punched me in the face then, but I do now. I dared him to try it a few years ago. Drift knows who I am. He drove me to see my real family, my Mom and Dad. He told me he hated my father when he was mad at me too. Oh how they loved to yell and scream at me all the time.

Every time I shared information about my Dad or real family, I was injured by Drift and Eva. I forgot everything when they hurt me. They hurt me to make sure I forgot my real parents and family. Just so my real parents know, they hurt me a lot and often. Don't worry about me, I am in good hands from above. I always have been and always will be. I am more than thankful for all the help I have received from above for my whole life, five decades and counting.

My bridge story is the first near death experience I was able to remember. The experience was a shock to me. This experience happened to me when I was fourteen years old just before my birthday in 1976. It took almost 40 years after experiencing the bridge event to be able to share all of this with anyone. Somehow I knew I could trust who visited me because they were familiar.

After my Mom's dad gave me to an orphanage, who in turn gave me over to an airplane pilot and stewardess, who in turn gave me over to Drift and Eva after my family didn't listen to me; what was I to believe in except Our Father in Heaven?

Our Father in Heaven is the only one I believe in and have faith in. He has always been there to help me. I know he will always be there for me and anyone else who asks for his help.

Now that I know what I know, I regained faith in my Dad. My Dad visited me in Arizona, Nevada and Wisconsin. I was dropped off at Dad's for a day, a weekend or longer sometimes. Drift would drive me because Eva did not drive until 1981. It has been fifty years since 1965

when I was eliminated from my family by my mother's father.

I had hoped my story might help my family to remember me. I have written to my Mom, her sister, her brother and my sister. I have received no reply. My sister wrote back to my girlfriend. Why could she not write back to me? I will no longer keep this a secret.

I kept it a secret because of the pain involved from my foster parents, Drift and Eva.

I kept it a secret because who was going to believe me? Even my own family didn't believe me.

I kept it a secret because I had no means of reaching my family.

I kept it a secret because I didn't know what to do when I was three years old.

The memories of my family came into focus and right back out of focus again until I turned forty years old. I was walking in my sleep from 1965 – 2001, thirty six years!

It took this long because it took this long.

Now that I know and I have no doubt, I know who to thank for getting my memories back, for being saved so many times and for knowing who saved me, Thank You. Let me expound a little on that in the next chapter.

Showing someone is better than telling them, isn't it?

CHAPTER ONE

What I Remembered From Our Father, I Am Forever Thankful

I would love to tell my story in perfect order, just like someone showed me quite a few times. Unfortunately, I do not have perfect recall, which is probably a good thing. Anyway, here I go!

I would like to thank my Mother and Father, Sister, Brothers, Great Grandmother, Grandma's and Grandpa's, Uncles and Aunts, Cousins and friends. Thank You to anyone else for visiting and trying to wake me up.

I would also like to thank my Classmates who tried to wake me up or who knew my story. Plenty of them knocked on our door and called me on the phone. I am glad you wanted to meet my Dad, he would have been happy to say hello to all of you. Thank you!

My real family was unknown to me. The whole concept of another family was unknown to me until the summer of 2001, I held a certain memory in high regard. I played 'Musical Chairs' and the game played in my head over and over for the whole summer. I believe it was playing somewhere in the background of my mind all the time.

How did I function for thirty six years of walking around in a sort of half-awake state-of-mind?

I was about to turn forty years old when I was saved again. I asked for my memories to come slower and it worked. That was in 2001 and it is 2015 now. Not only does it take some time to remember and write it down, it also takes time to continue earning a living and supporting my family and myself. Has anyone noticed how much everything costs? I have sticker shock.

WAKING UP

I was punished for being aggressive while playing 'Musical Chairs'. I was in kindergarten.

I pushed my way into a chair when the music stopped. A girl was trying for the same chair. I was trying to be gentle, but I was trying to 'win' and the girl did not hit the seat of the chair as solid as I did. She bounced off of me a few times while I was sitting in the chair. She was being aggressive, not me. My punishment was no lunch and writing something like, "I will not hurt others when we are playing games", on the blackboard.

I was tired of school in kindergarten.

I saw an open window and pushed a chair over to it. I pushed the window open a little more and crawled out. I was hungry and nothing fun happened in the classroom anyway. The teacher always punished me for every little thing. She did not understand that I never got to play with other kids. I was no longer interested in school because it was not fun. We hardly ever played and when we did it was for a few minutes. It was time to leave school behind when I was three, maybe four years old. I know I am not alone with this thought.

MY MEMORIES

I ran away on Christmas Eve and hitch hiked away from my moms' family when I found out they did not want to raise me. They would not let me be part of Christmas with them, it hurt.

I used to 'spy' on our neighbors. I used a periscope and grandma's opera glasses. I would take a ladder and prop it up against the fence and use the periscope first. I was play acting and mimicking what I saw on television shows. I wanted to report the news! One can only imagine how my family took that phone call or knock at the door. I know how they took it quite directly.

I used the electric pruning shears to practice 'topiary' on the shrubs. The artwork was somewhat appreciated given my age. Delivery was swift to guide me to make a better choice the next time I saw any power tool.

I used grandpa's wax seal to send a letter to my Dad. I sat at my grandpa's desk and typed a letter. I added some handwritten part and signed it. Like Grandpa, I wanted to seal this important document so my Dad would get it without anyone reading it first. My adventure took a turn for the worse when the candle to heat the wax was tipped over. I threw it and the burning mat from the desk into the trash can next to the desk. The flames got higher and the fire department was called. I was no longer allowed in that room or to play with matches.

I was trapped under the garage door. It caught me when I kept rolling under it to show off. One time it caught me. I only remember waking up numb from whatever happened to me. A little more sugar and medicine in a spoon and off to sleep for me.

I wanted to start the lawn mower because I liked the sound of the engine running. Instead of sitting and listening to the running engine, I took our riding tractor mower for a ride when I turned the key. I drove haphazardly through grandma's garden, shrubs, and backyard in general. How was I to know it was in gear? Oh the things everyone yelled at me while my Dad caught up to me and kept getting shocked trying to turn off the engine. He turned the key to off as he was running alongside the moving mower, but the mower kept going. The mower kept going because it had to be turned off by grounding out the spark plug. As the mower was moving, it was bumpy and hard to hold on to, bouncing over the bumpy terrain. Grounding out the spark plug to shut it off was harder than it should have been because I could not reach the brake to stop the machine. Dad was getting shocked pretty good. He did manage to stop the engine, jolted as he was, he was pretty nice to me. He did talk to me though. No more sitting on the riding lawn mower.

I played the record player and grabbed a baton from the conductor's stand and directed music playing on the record player. It became a little intense and so did my conducting! It became a problem because I was not supposed to be in Grandma and Grandpa's bedroom. Not to mention, "The no jumping or directing on the bed rule". I didn't know they had a rule against jumping and conducting on a bed?

I know I took one of Dad's friends for a drive in one of our cars. I grabbed the keys from the key rack and we started the car and went for a drive. Dad's friend was so excited that we were able to, "Go for a spin". I told him to go slower or faster, stop and go, turn right or left. He was at the wheel and loving every second of it. We did real good for most of our trip until we hit a fire plug. What a mess! I didn't know what blind was until Dad explained it to me. I left the key rack alone after that chat.

I wanted a dragline for my birthday, but mostly I wanted a day with my Dad. He promised me a baseball game around my birthday, depending on the Dodgers schedule. I would wake up every morning more excited than the day before hoping it would be the day he could take me to a baseball game.

The day he was supposed to take me to a game, we went to the auto parts store. We called it, 'the drag shop". He introduced me to a guy named 'Drift'. Circa 1965, the game and the day are well documented. 'Drift' took me to the game along with a kid named 'Mike'.

I know this really happened because I was there. My Dad and I went to the drag shop. My Dad was done and we went to the car in the parking ramp. I asked if I could shift the car and my Dad let me. The car did not go into reverse however, it went forward and off the second level parking ramp from where we were parked.

I tried to drag my Dad out of the car. He was heavy.

Shortly after this accident, my Dad gave Drift money every month.

OH HOW I WISH I COULD TAKE THAT MOMENT AND MISTAKE BACK.

Wrong Field, wrong game, wrong teams, wrong Dad but Dad was hurt. Twins won the first of two and we left after the first game to a camping tent rental place. The rented tent was placed into the trunk. Drift dropped off the other boy and took me to the desert. I played along.

BAD DECISIONS LEAD TO MORE BAD DECISIONS.

I survived living in the desert for a long time with no tent, no water and no food. I was very angry with my Dad when this ordeal was over. However, it was only the beginning.

I would run away from Drift and Eva's house to my real home, or to a police phone on a pole. I would call my parents if I had money, but money, even a nickel, was hard to come by for my age. When the police picked me up, they took me back to Drift and Eva's.

GOOD THINGS

I have all these cards I wrote my memories down on to share with my son and my real family. Here they are in and out of order:

Musical Chairs- My first memory that led me back to my real family. Both playing the game and understanding the concept. Imagine playing a game of elimination knowing you are being eliminated from your family. Imagine remembering your real family and having to compare families to see if you are correct or not. It is how I figured things out.

My School Uniform- I had a uniform that all the boys wore every day for school.

Bringing the teacher an apple to let her know I was sorry I left the classroom without letting her know. My teacher was not appreciative and I was also sorry I went back to school. My folks talked me into it.

My Great Grandmother- Who laid out my school uniform and all my other outfits prior and after school. Whistling teapot, washing and drying clothes, ice cream cones, pedal car, home sweet home. I called her Nana. Nana taught me how to survive. She took care of our family.

My Grandparents- Grandma stayed in her room or went into town. She ate at the table but mostly passed on eating. Grandma's symbol is her vanity mirror and all her perfume bottles. Grandpa's symbol was his size. His presence was that he was very large! He was not so much tall, wide would be a better way to describe him. However, being physically large was not Grandpa's strong suit, it was more so his demeanor. When Grandpa opened the door to the house, dinner was ready for Grandpa.

Grandma and Grandpa always asked each other permission, like for smoking. Grandpa sometimes went into the 'smoking room' and he put on his smoking jacket, got out his pipe rack, pulled out the humidor and then he searched for the right pouch that smelled just right to upset Grandma. After he lit up, he would ask if it was okay to smoke.

Grandma on the other hand, had her special selection of cigars that she smoked to make sure and balance the horrible smells in the house. You don't mind if I join you she would ask grandpa.

When Grandpa came home after work. he would slide his shoes off his feet and I would slide our ottoman under his feet. I handed him the newspaper, the mail, whatever he wanted. I treated him nice.

I stopped using the bathroom upstairs because mom and her brother and sister had to use the bathroom before school. I was just learning how to use the toilet! So I reverted back to crawling around and pissing my diaper or pants while everyone else used the bathroom. Great grandma noticed and let me use her bathroom. Please note, at this time, only my great grandma stuck up for me. Everyone else was too busy to know I was alive. My Mom tried, so did her sister, but they were busy too. They still can't see me. This is what my mom tells me when I call her. I stopped calling her. Why should I try so hard when she has not tried for my whole life to call me. Because my Dad tried so hard to reach me and I didn't even know he was my Dad.

Because my Dad never gave up on me. He visited me and he took care of me.

Later on my Dad visited us and threw Drift and Eva in Lake Havasu. I know you threw them in the lake because you knew what they were doing to me. Nevada Kidd knew what Drift and Eva were doing to me, they tortured me. Nevada is my Dad, you see I found out who you were when Drift and Eva walked by me cursing you! Both of them cursed you. First Eva walked by.

"Your fucking Dad threw me in the lake!" Eva went on and on about how my father threw her in the lake, so I thought Drift threw her in the lake. It didn't make sense that Drift threw her in the lake because he knew she was afraid of the water. Drift is afraid of the water too.

Not even a minute later Drift walked by me soaking wet. He said the same thing to me, Drift was really mad at me. "Your Fucking Dad threw me in the lake!" He went on and on.

I stood there a minute and was confused. I saw Eva walk by soaking wet and cursing my Dad. Drift walked by soaking wet and they both said my Dad threw them in the lake! I was really blocking everything out then. Drift and Eva gave away the truth when they were confronted by my Dad, the Nevada Kidd. Dad brought me a glow football and we played catch in the dark. Nevada and I played catch a lot, so did Arizona and I.

Arizona is my son.

It was 1969 and my Dad tried to take me home. I was scared. I wasn't myself. When you left they made me suffer a whole lot more than ever before. Eva had her other son, or nephew or whatever tie me up and piss on me. His name is Suzie Cumdumpster. He was trying to make me do something I will never do for any man. I bit him where it hurts and he left me alone. I taught him a lesson. It must have been my turn.

I am still alive in body and soul.

God Bless Our Father in Heaven, God Bless My Father and the fact that he was trying to show me how he felt. He stood up for me just like I stood up for my son Arizona.

What you did was much appreciated. It took me a long time to snap out of it. I figured out what you did for me thirty six years later. Thank You Dad! I love you.

My father visited me and I visited him for many years behind the scenes. He knew to come to me one-on-one. At first he came to see me with his father and his brother. We played music together. We each took a turn playing one of the accordions Grandpa brought along. After playing the accordions, Grandpa brought out his ukulele and Dad brought out his guitar. My uncle played instruments too, but mostly he just sang along. They asked me if I could yodel. They had to give me an example. I started to do it and then, 'I yodeled' and it was a big deal to them. I can still yodel if that means anything. Grandpa said, "The Kidd's got it!"

I received toys from a delivery truck from my family. Drift and Eva gave all of them to their families. I received a white gardenia quite often at this house. Drift and Eva told me it was their flower from their friends. They would not let me remember my own family no matter what. They would not let me enjoy anything from them.

That was in a Las Vegas suburb around fall of 1965. Maurice, David and my Dad Nevada used to come by quite often at that time. Drift had to drive me to see them and it pissed him off. Drift always took his anger out on me. Drift made me get on the floor of the car every time. He made me get down on the floor in the backseat of his car. If my head popped up, he hit it.

I visited a house in town. We played above the garage in that house. I think this was the one with a pool in the garage. This one also had a stairway into the living room where the twins played in a play pen after they were born. I used to change the twins diapers, I had to take them upstairs to the changing table. My sister helped me move them around, they were heavy! Mom was on the phone with her hair all bunched up under a towel. She was never to concerned about us. She was concerned with her nails, her hair and her looks. She was worried how she looked.

There was a house on the beach. The coffee table had a glass sheet on the top. Underneath the sheet of glass was a seascape that was extremely detailed. Downstairs was the bathroom and mostly an open space to the sliding door. You opened the sliding door to get down to the beach. This was my grandparent's house on Lake Havasu. Clear water to see through and cold.

We were in Lake Havasu in Arizona. Lake Havasu has a mobile home park at the north end of town right on the beach. Even though I was on the floor of the car and would get punished when I looked, I did peek to see where I was when I could. So what if I got smacked. I knew where I was at all times by looking.

I saw the mobile home park. I knew we were on the way to my family, when I saw the mobile home park and I knew we were real close after our drive from the other side of the river. I always felt better with my family. Getting closer to them helped me feel better too.

I saw my family again and stayed many times at the beach house. I played with my sister on the beach. I set up bottles because they would sing in the wind.

My sister, Lady wanted me to put my handprints in the cement at this house.

My handprints are possibly still in the cement walkway by the steps to the front or side door. I know the city quite well now. Back then in 1965 or so, the artist's took over a somewhat abandoned lumber yard. My mother would take me there. She would visit with the artist's and I would entertain myself by climbing the incredibly unique brick walls, walk around the old lumberyard and talk to other artist's, play with the carved sailboats in a tub and just walked around. The lumberyard building is still there. Now it is a combination office building, retail and a restaurant. I had a drink with a guy named Jimmy there in 2005 the first week of January.

There was a ranch house. It had a living room full of suits of armor. I'm not sure, but this may have been the house where we watched wild horses, played in canyons and drove around in the Ford Bronco. I'm not clear on where this house was located. We turned by a jeep.

Another ranch house where Mom took us too and this one was a long drive to get there. We played my sister's match game called 'Simple-Simon' or something like that all the way there. They had pool's inside and outside and all sizes. We stayed in one of the two houses by the really big old ranch house. There was an old pool with old statues around it.

There was another house where Dad did his wrenching. The garage door was an automatic door. Dad had his tool chests in the garage. Dad could blow smoke rings and this is where he did it best!

There was a lodge cabin in the mountains. We went there when it was snowing and went skiing, snowmobiling, tobogganing, and the lodge had an old fashioned crank phone. This cabin had a very special toilet. We sat around the fireplace and shared memories and stories.

There was my Mom's parents' houses. One in town, brick on the front. One house had a garden in the back for Grandma and great Grandma, a big bow window to sit in, a basement and only one bathroom upstairs for kids and one we couldn't use in Grandma and Grandpa's room. The other house had a pool, a poolside glass room, a golf course, a sports room downstairs and its own putting green!

You would have thought my Grandfather was going to heaven because he had a putting green in his backyard. He was a simple man. My Grandpa on my Mom's side is Gorilla McGillicudy, they called him the Ape. He was so happy to move to his new house with a putting green in the back yard. They called him the Grape Ape.

I went there on rare occasion. No one welcomed me at this house.

Once my uncle played tether ball with me at this house. Remember Uncle? Wasn't that you? I beat you at tether ball and it ticked you off. A little hot headed weren't we? Nana helped unravel me from the tether ball pole. You know, after you tied me up to it with the tether ball rope? I always knew you were wound a little tight! Want to play a game of tetherball now? I play games with people who understand the rules now. If you don't understand the rules, I can show you! My uncle was smaller than grandpa and they called him the Chimp. He didn't like me because his Dad, the Ape, didn't like me.

I hope you had a change of heart.

I believe my Grandparents had a place in Las Vegas too. Really nice house.

Mom's Folks and my Grandparents had homes in 'gated' communities. When Drift dropped me off, he had to talk to a guard in the guardhouse and get the okay to go through the gate.

We had to do the same thing in Wisconsin at my Dad's house in North Birch Lakes. We had to stop and check in at the gate. Drift checked in at the gate and we went to the right. When we saw the golf course we took a left and drove to the pillars. I only saw the pillars just off the road to mark the driveway, the garage and then the back of the house. Why? Because Drift always had me get down on the floor of the car in the backseat, remember? I peeked when I could, but would get punished if I got caught peaking to long. This house is on East Birch Lakes Drive. I know the house quite well now. I found it when I was on a landscape design call in 1985. I drove back and forth in front of it and then I went back again. I sensed an attachment, but had no idea why the house was so familiar to me. I drove by the house again in 2001 and knew the pillars which still stand today in 2015! What a great feeling it was to drive in the driveway, squat down like I was in the late 1960's, and see the same two pillars marking a memory for me! The gates and guard at the guard shack are long gone now.

I remember all the bottle cap art my Dad was putting together at this house.

There was the house in Arizona where Dad played music. The bathroom shower had a sliding glass door. There was a drum set, a trombone on a stand, a sax, a flute, music stands, a piano and a closet full of trophy's. When you opened the closet door, the trophies fell all over.

Another house with my captain's bed and my pet turtle. I would leave my captain's wheel light on at night. Even early on when I was a smaller child, I left a light on at night! My Dad called me the 'Moth'. This was the house where we were all going to live together again. I have no idea where it is.

Another house with 'topiary' in front. This house was the house with a piano and a humidifier. The house and the whole neighborhood was on a hill. I found a garden-in-a-can on top of the refrigerator and wanted to throw the seeds on the hill to protect us from erosion, ha! I wonder if my sister remembers racing to the car so the winner could ride shotgun? We fought over who could sit next to you Dad because we both love you!

Then there were Grandpa's houses. His main house was on a hill. You went by an airport, in fact, right by the airport light tower. He had a Russian Olive in front of the house. He showed family movies inside. He had violets growing under lights. He threw parties there. The deck had a tree growing in it! He didn't want to cut the tree down, but he had no problem trimming branches! I say this because I was pruned from our family tree. Morrie is what Drift called my grandpa. It was my Grandpa Maurice.

There are even more houses, apartments and places I have been that my family owned or rented. This is a list of the homes that I stayed at or visited for any length of time. There is an apartment with a clock that read 25 or 6 to 4, but it was a modern clock with banks of lights instead of hands. Dad said when I could tell him the right time on the clock, he would give me a surprise. This is how my Dad talked to me. I remember things like this with music. The time on the clock that day may or may not have been the afore mentioned time. Since there is a song with this name, it is how I choose to remember the moment in time with my Dad, through music.

There is an apartment that my Mom lived at for a short time. It is where she lived when she took art classes. Grandpa came and took Mom home from there. He took me with, but only because he needed time to think about what to do with me. He made that real clear.

I liked when my Mom took me to her art classes. The teacher accepted my presence unwillingly. The teacher was worried about me being there when the subject matter was a nude. So my Mom had me play behind her work station. He was nothing to look at anyway. Some of the paintings were pretty far out there. It is always interesting to me how people interpret what they see, or hear, or perceive.

I was busy playing with my farm set toys while my Mom painted. Pretend land was more familiar to me then some guy who couldn't afford clothes. It was nice to know he was paid for sitting there without clothes knowing he would soon have money to get clothes. I think my Mom told me this story, it made me feel better.

I wonder if my Mom remembers me watching everyone fuss with her wedding dress?

I wonder if my Mom remembers taking me to be sized for a blue velvet suit and hat to wear to her wedding?

I wonder if my mom remembers me looking thought the keyhole of her bedroom door?

I wonder if my Mom remembers helping me write letters to my Dad and then mailing them?

I wonder if my Mom remembers taking me to the candy store? To the London Bridge?

I wonder if my Mom remembers taking Sister and I to the beach in the wagon?

Picnic baskets full of pre-made sandwiches, tuna salad, chicken salad, cheese and more..

Picnic basket with red and white bottle holders on the beach. My time alone with you and Dad.

I wonder if my Mom remembers me at her wedding?

I did not take the pearl necklace and I do not care who did it either. When I was young and still living with Gorilla and Jane McGillicudy, my Mothers folks, someone planted a pearl necklace in my dresser drawer. I was three years old and hardly a jewel thief.

I can go on and on and on and on and on.

My Dad tried to give me a really nice mini bike in Menomonie Wisconsin at the park where we were camping. There used to be an outdoor theater there. He was driving an old panel van and wearing a tan suede leather jacket with really long fringe over it. He had really long hair.

My Dad used to visit me out-of-the-blue. He would just be standing there when I walked on my paper route. That is when he took me for a ride in a jet boat docked by Lord Fletchers Apartments on Lake Havasu. Another time I was walking in Penn Park in Wisconsin and he showed up with his brother. We played catch and he pitched a baseball to me. I hit the ball real good! Like I said, Dad and I played catch all the time. Drift played catch with me once. He threw the football at me as hard as he could and I still caught it. He threw it three times. He was around all the time and played catch with me three times, less than my Dad did. My Dad showed up a few times a year when he could. He always apologized he couldn't come by more often. He watched me play football as I grew up. He always loved me.

Dad tried to tell me over and over about what happened, but I was mad at him and everyone responsible for not listening to me when I told them the people they gave me to were hurting me. Plus I was afraid all the time. Drift and Eva never let up on me, they were constantly yelling at me because they knew how much it bothered me.

I do not talk to the people that raised me now and have not since 2005. Hopefully all the seeds they have sewn have come to fruition. I remember what Eva, Drift and some of their family members did to me because of Our Father in Heaven. What Eva, Drift and most of their relatives did to me is unforgiven. There are very few exceptions and they know who they are, thank you for helping. I know how hard it is to function while walking in my sleep, so I know it was hard for you to share any information with me while walking around in your sleep.

Before I remembered any of this Arizona was born. I named him and agreed his middle name should be Waldemar after his Mother's Father. Arizona looks like our Dad, more than me even, he is tall too. It is funny to think Arizona is unsure of his background. I have tried to tell him. He believes me but his Mom deters him. Chicago is Arizona's Mom. Chicago knows the story because I told her my story, but Chicago does not believe me and is amongst many in Chapter Five, which is reserved for the unbeliever's.

There is a place for everyone. It is her decision. She never believed anything I said, it is why I left her.

Arizona has the same abilities as I have and you should hear his voice. Both Arizona and I are shy to sing out. We still sing quite often. It was more than unpleasant to sing with Drift and Eva for me. They are so tone deaf that it hurts my ears to be near them while they are singing.

The gifts given to Arizona and I at birth were not fostered so that we could grow in a natural way. We overcame the obstacles presented to us and will continue to overcome obstacles until our mission is accomplished. We will accomplish our mission with or without our families help because our help comes from above anyway. It would be nice to see you all and introduce Arizona as you could introduce yourselves and your children. It is your choice.

My Father's family made an effort to visit me. I can only wonder about the rest of my family. I wonder if any of you will decide to see me or believe in me when the time comes? For now I have to wonder why you stopped trying and focus on how strong my Dad was for trying.

MORE MEMORIES

My Father wanted to have music around me. Dad had a night set aside for us to get together and play music. I remember playing the drums at one of these events. Others joined me and it was my first jam. The next week, someone attached wood blocks to the drum pedals so I could reach them easier.

One of these music nights, Drift drove home and crashed his car.

One of these nights we all did the limbo.

One of these nights I got up on stage during the band break and played the drums.

One of these nights I met a lady with hand cymbals.

One of these nights was a Halloween Night, some of us wore costumes. Remember the guy with the trench coat and rubber mask over his head?

One of these nights of playing music we sang G-L-O-R-I-A!

FOR MY SISTER, LADY SLIPPER KIDD

Playing games with you. Play acting with you. The swing at Grandpa's other house and the tree in the deck. Do you remember the deck built around the tree at Grandpa's house? When he had a tea party, we played on a swing. Do you remember rocking back and forth on the swing?

We lived on a hill, I wanted to throw the garden-in-a-can seeds on the hill to keep it from eroding. This is the house with the humidifier I had to fill with water. We did this to keep the instruments from drying out.

Snorkeling to find things. Flippers made it easy to swim. Skipping stones.

Grandpa Maurice told me and my sister we were like book ends, just like our twin brothers. It was not nice to separate us.

The pedal car. Ice cream cone variety at Grandma's. Gated entry to this house.

Do you remember the disguises everyone wore when you visited? Ha! One time my Mom, Dad and sister picked me up in a VW station wagon. You were all wearing Groucho Marx masks. I wish I wasn't walking around in my sleep back then. I am laughing now and happy you went to great lengths to get my attention. Thanks for the nice lunch and for spending time with me.

My sister came to visit me by taxi cab. You told me we will always be blood brother and sister. Thank you for believing in me! Your promise was a fantastic verification for me when I began to remember. I am guessing your memory of me is long gone since you do not reply to my letters to you via Facebook. Nice of you to write back asking Faith about me. It would have been nicer if you wrote to me, but it has also been 47 years. I will see you in Heaven, you will recognize me then. Of course you have to get there first. Good Luck!

'Cinnamon' is the color of your hair, just like the color of my hair.

You had another agenda to fulfill that day too. Do you remember your plan when I had to move to Wisconsin? You wanted me to leave popcorn or some trail for you and Dad to follow. Now you do not need to follow a trail, I can give you directions or visit you. Call first of course.

Diamond Jim starts to visit me. He drives a cool old truck. It was an Apache. We drive around because it is our favorite thing to do. I met Jim at my Mom's house. I saw him through the keyhole when my Mom would not answer her door. They let me in unwillingly. I would not have made a fuss but I had a nightmare.

I remember my Mom's fake belly made of foam. She kept it under the bed and wore it to look pregnant with my sister who was already born.

My captains bed and captains wheel light. This bedroom was beige, blue and brown plaid. I had a pet turtle. This bedroom was nice because I did not share it with anyone like at Drift and Eva's house. I had my own bed. At Drift and Eva' house, I had to sleep next to their kid in the same bed until I was in third grade.

My visits to grandpa's office. His office had a bunch of girls at desks and special two piece 'solo' coffee cups. They were a plastic cup bottom that you could put a plastic insert cup in it and it clicked when they were together. You put them together and threw away the plastic insert instead of having to wash them. Maurice always had a water cooler at his office and at his houses too. Maurice's house is also vivid in my memory.

Maurice's other house where Grandma lived with the player piano and player piano roll storage room. All alphabetized! The piano tuner man and his neat forks. He tuned both piano's. There was a baby grand along with the player piano in the music room.

Maurice showed me how to cut and splice film at his office To do this I had to learn how to load his special projector. He showed me how to make sound effects. He showed me the dark room.

One time I walked in on him in the dark room and he was upset, but never so mad that he hurt me like my foster parents. He would talk to me about things except when I sat in his director's chair. Everyone told me not to, but I thought he would be okay with it.

I lived at the Kidd house in town on Palomino Horse Drive for a short time. I slept in my Uncles old room. It was my Grandpa's way of trying to make things right. My Grandpa and my Dad had an argument about me. My Dad was not happy about what my other Grandpa (My Mom's Dad) did to me. At first my Dad thought Maurice was in on it, but now my Dad was happier about how Grandpa was trying to get to know me. Maurice and Charlotte loved me a lot and told me so. They said they loved me all the time. Grandpa always said, "The Kid's got it."

Grandpa opened a court case to get me back. He called it a paternity suit or case.

Knowing this makes it obvious to me that My Dad's side of my family "Loved and Cared" about me. I finally figured this out recently. This is a project that has taken me fourteen years to put together.

I wanted to make sure this information was right. I have the information verified by another author and a friend of our family, Sharon Seesme. Sharon was very close to our family.

I do not doubt Our Father in Heaven. I am honoring my promise because he honors his promises.

Maurice taught me a lot in a very short amount of time. I told him I learned through osmosis.

He laughed and was really happy with that joke. "The kid has it" he said. just by being around my Grandpa. He was not an ordinary man and in some ways, it was hard to understand how he could accomplish everything he did in one day. My Dad's Dad was the busiest man I have ever known and no one would disagree with me.

He wrote things down on his typewriter in his home office.

He met with a lot of people every day at the house and at his office in town.

He liked talking to the girls in his office. He liked to ask them how all the mail was coming along. Grandpa received mailbags at his office. The bags were stacked up outside by the entry doors on the side street of the building. There were always 10-12 bags of mail or more when I visited. I had to move them out of the way so Drift could open the door.

My Grandma Jane explains life to me before I was given away by my Grandfather. Grandma tells me about plants, animals and bugs. She said I am like the praying mantis. Oddly enough, this is what my other Grandma Charlotte told me.

When we left for Wisconsin in 1968, my Grandma is following us in a Rambler! My Grandma and her friend followed us when we left to go to Wisconsin. My Grandma and her friend had the same two Bobble Head dolls in the back window of the Rambler. It is how I recognized her and her friend. I love you Grandma, thank you for keeping in touch with me for so long.

They visited me in Wisconsin in 1980 too!

These were the same two that visited me in Wisconsin. Charlotte and her friend and I talked about Dutchman's Breeches, Jack in the Pulpit, and why the trees grew the way they did in the woods. When they visited we talked about plants just like we did when I was little!

The difference was the state we were in and that I told them what I learned about plants.

I did not see if they still had the Bobble Heads because I didn't see their car. Drift and Eva were upset at seeing them and made a scene so they left. Before they left, they said they were proud of me and loved what I knew about flowers. I kind of knew we were connected but didn't know how at the time. I was still in a walking sleep in 1980.

Moving from one part of Lake Havasu to another part of Lake Havasu in 1966. Smaller place, further away and some of the weirdest memories of all time. Beach Boys music playing in the house across the way, all the time. You could hear the music all the time because her windows were open all the time.

IN MY ROOM – BEACH BOYS

The two kids next door, Missy and her little brother. The teenage girls, sisters that were our baby sitters. Their Mom was a seamstress at Disneyland.

Maurice and Charlotte are staying in a house along the way to my school. The school is Cactus Flower Elementary in Lake Havasu. I do not remember the exact address of their house, but I know it was in between where I lived and the school. Grandma came out of the house and into the yard when I walked by after school. She invited me in and I accepted. Grandma tells me to make myself at home. I did. Grandpa was sick. He was wearing his Boy Scout medallion, which he wore when he was down. There was something wrong with his kidney's or liver. They asked me to invite my friends by for an after school snack so I brought Chuck by one day to meet them. Chuck knew who they were. They were well known.

Dad came by and was talking to me through the fence on the east side of our school. I was in my sleep walking frame of mind and pulled the fire alarm and the fire department showed up. I was scared and confused, please forgive me Dad? The newspaper and TV people did not stop calling and knocking at our door. Drift and Eva were furious and covered all our windows with fake snow spray, cardboard and anything they could find. They unplugged the phone and punished me to no end until we moved.

We had to move again because to many people were beginning to figure out my real families identity. This was in May of 1968 right before we moved in June, before school let out. It was my Dad's folks and I was happy to see them, but I was in my walking sleep.

The house in between the Walker's and my school is where Charlotte cut my hair. She was very concerned that we would be separated and she wanted to make sure it was me when we met again. I suggested cutting my hair after we talked about it. Even Grandpa thought it was a good idea. He was being really nice to me at that time, Grandma too. Grandma opened a drawer and pulled out a big scissors. She reached into a drawer and pulled out an envelope. She clipped some of my hair and put it into the labeled envelope.

One of my High School Teachers, Julius, told me, "Someday it will all come back to you". Julius loved the Rolling Stones. I cannot prove anything, but I think Julius met with my Dad. Julius took me to the Wisconsin Orchestra and a nice filet mignon dinner for Taking Care of Business for him. One day a year our vocational school had an open house to introduce what the school programs were. I introduced the Horticulture program and Julius had a full classroom the following year. He said he never received such a positive response!

Julius is my favorite teacher!

COMPARISONS THAT I MADE AFTER I WOKE UP

I compared my first memories and the people I lived with before living with Drift and Eva.

Drift and Eva did not re-enroll me in my private school. Public school instead.

Drift and Eva put my sandwich in a brown paper bag. No lunchbox anymore.

Drift and Eva took away my raincoat, boots and hat. I walked to school wet if it rained.

Drift and Eva gave me no love, no caring and absolutely no compassion.

Drift and Eva tortured, beat and brainwashed me to block out my family on purpose.

Drift and Eva enjoyed hurting me when I was a three year old and on, they even laughed at me.

Drift and Eva gave away all my toys to their families.

Eva did not drive a car until 1981, my Mom always drove a car.

Every time I try to compare Drift and Eva to my family, they fail! I had to wake up first to be able to understand all of this.

Now to compare my great Grandmother with the one Drift and Eva presented in her place.

My Nana! My great-Great Grandma lived with my Mom's folks when I was little. She fed me, cleaned me, showed me how to play, read to me, explained things to me. Her teapot would start whistling in the morning, it was our families alarm clock. I lived at the top of the stairs by the bathroom. Nana read Bible stories to me. She loved me and cared about me more than anyone else except my Dad's family.

As soon as we moved to Wisconsin, Drift and Eva took me to see their dead great grandmother. I thought it was my Nana. It was part of their plan to twist what happened to them and use it to disrupt me in any way. That was their main concern. Disrupt, Divert and Devastate Me!

I remember the adults talking about what to do with me. Great Grandma said they would regret their decision. The decision was made and carried out by my Grandfather, mom's dad. He took me to an orphanage. I remember the black car, the black mood, the black day.

PAINT IT BLACK – THE ROLLING STONES

One boy at the orphanage protected me because he wanted out of the orphanage. He asked me to pretend he was my older brother. He wanted to live in a home with a family. I tried as hard as I could to help him, but no one believed me.

Lots of kids living at the orphanage were deformed or damaged by thalidomide. The kids who were functional wanted to get out of there in the worst way. I wanted to help them so much but I also had to protect myself. I had no way of helping them then, but I can help now. I hope my book helps people understand that children have no rights. Pets have more rights than children.

I was called bad names by my Mom's dad For some reason, I think of this Grandpa as Moses. Moses did not like bastards either. You can read what Moses wrote in the Bible.

My Mom's name is Brandy. Brandy McGillicuddy. Do you remember telling me to call you by your first name instead of Mom? Brandy is your new first name. Charlotte told me your real name was like a bottle of Brandy. Charlotte showed me a bottle of Brandy to show me how it was spelled. I had a Mom with so many first names it is a miracle I remembered any of them. I'm no longer confused. My Mom's name is Brandy Bottle. Brandy McGillicudy.

I had to call everyone by their first name now in the McGillicudy house. Nana didn't go along with Gorilla's demands. In the Kidd house, I was asked to call them by their title and name so I would feel connected. Like Grandpa Maurice or Grandma Charlotte etc. God Bless my family.

No more great Grandma Nana, No more Grandpa Gorilla or Grandma Jane.

No more McGillicudy's to visit because they never wanted to see me again. Nana is the exception. I saw my Mom when I was visiting my Dad, but she didn't care.

I didn't even know your first names. Isn't it odd I know your faces? I had to learn your names. How many kids know their parents' first names at three years old?

My Mom and her sister had a playroom with their two rocking horses in the corner. I played with my Uncles toys which were very neatly stacked on shelves behind sliding closet doors. My favorite toys were the farm animals inside a fold open barn.

My Dominoes! I set them up to watch them go with very little effort.

I am wondering if my Mom was the baton twirler or was it her sister, or maybe both?

I am wondering if my Mom remembers under the stairway, where the fake rifle and batons were stored? I wonder if my Mom's Sister or Brother remember? I don't think the McGillicudy's want to remember me. Except for Nana. In 1965 and on, visits to the McGillicudy's were few and not fun.

THE BAD NEWS HALLOWEEN PARTY.

I remember the visits to the costume shop with Mom and sister so we could pick out costumes. My Mom put me in a devil costume with a pitchfork. When guests arrived, I hid under the coats on the big bed at the Halloween Party. I was into my hiding mood because I am not the devil. Because I knew the McGillicudy's elimination plan. I was in a bad mood. Mom made a horrible choice to put me in a devil costume.

How would you like to know your own Grandfather gave you to an orphanage to protect his place in society, or was it to get into another gated community?. I think you know what I think of you Gorilla McGillicudy. I told you what I thought of you before you rid yourself of a three year old. Watch out for the pitchfork, not mine though, mine is a costume accessory.

Playing hangman with my sister. It is a word game. Playing under the pyramid. Playing under the teepee. My Sister and I played pretty good together until she had girlfriends.

I sang a lullaby to my sister when she was in a bassinet just home from the hospital.

My good grandparents had a man for everything! A piano tuner man, the pool man, milk man, garbage man, lawn mower men, mailman, a doctor made house visits man, a carpenter man, a diaper service man; even a young man to deliver the papers, not a paper man, a paperboy! They had a lot of people working for them at an office somewhere too. A mailman again, a window cleaner man, a maintenance man, a sound effects man, a light man, a make-up man, a wardrobe man (or woman), Humphrey Man in the orchestra, men in the orchestra, set man, food and beverage man, a man for everything. Let's not forget the office girls keeping track of the mail. There was a whole floor of women with typewriters on their desks replying to the mail.

I used to read the Encyclopedia Britannica to learn things. I read the statistics about which state was best to live in. I chose where to live because people lived longer in Wisconsin and Hawaii.

We went to the Renaissance Fair in Arizona! Bad news for me, I was put in the yokes. This was a bad day for me. Dad was mad at Mom. Mom was mad at me. This is when Dad found out about Diamond Jim through the keyhole. I was only talking about what I had been doing and Jim came up. My Dad did not like Jim and did not like me talking about him.

Mom and Dad's big wedding Day. My Mom had me fitted for a blue velvet suit and matching hat for this wonderful occasion. My Grandma drove me to my other Grandparent's house. Grandpa had us shining our shoes and looking good. He put cufflinks in my shirt cuffs and a bowtie in my collar. I looked great and I felt great, I was with my own kind. Grandpa asked me how I looked, I said I looked grand. "The kid's got it," he said.

Grandpa put his hat on the back of his head and gave me one of his hats we wore on the back of our heads. The boys put their hats on the same way and we prayed before we left.

Great Grandma picked me up a little after that and we went to the wedding in time to throw rice. Great Grandma said no one would notice with all the mayhem going on, so she gave me some rice to throw for my Mom and Dad. It was our turn to throw rice when my folks walked by. I kept a straight face and let the rice fly out of my hand. Dad winked at me. Wink back. I tied some old shoes to the bumper to your escape vehicle thanks to help from uncle, Dad's brother.

I threw rice at the wedding thanks to my great Grandma! She took me to the reception and I created a scene at the wedding reception. I was crawling around the tables looking for my Mom! I was not trying to create a scene! I just missed my Mom.

"We will be tarred and feathered, We will be run out of this town," I kept wondering why all this chaos over me? In 1966, a lot of people lost their jobs. I heard this from my Grandpa Maurice at first. "Life as we know it is over". The Maurice and Charlotte Show, the longest running show in Las Vegas, was over in 1966. Maurice was very sad that the casino let the show go. No watch, no Thank You, just good bye. It is a fact that no one knows to this day why the show was cancelled. Something happened to cancel the show. What could the something be?

Who would know why the show was cancelled?

I know why.

My Grandfather Gorilla, checked out to Chapter Five for unbelievers. Maurice made a decision to accept me. I didn't understand any of this until recently. I sure am sad about what one Grandfather did to me. The other one is a shining example of an "old dog learning new tricks". That is what Maurice told me. Grandma had a way of persuading Grandpa. Grandpa had a way of persuading everybody else. I love and miss you all.

My Grandma Jane showed me the attic and the treasures in her hope chest or trunk.

Great Grandpa Merlin! I loved your painting of the ship. I am most like you Merlin. I know you were also a Jack-Of-All-Trades. We are both blessed by Our Father in Heaven. I paint, did mosaics, sing, drum, play guitar, write, fight, and I stand up for my own kind. I can wrench, hammer, destroy, repair, and I can work in an office for short periods of time.

I think I had a race car bed? I vaguely remember a race car theme for my room.

Mostly I love my family even when they do not love me.

When my Mom first moved out of her parents' home, we lived in a high rise apartment building. I could see the numbers from high above on buses and trucks.

I remember turning the escalator off to save a girl that was getting pulled in by one.

Mom, Dad and Sister took me to a high place with a telescope. I remembered this because Drift and Eva never put any money in telescopes because it was a waste of money. My folks said how much do you need? It was okay to pay and view a long ways away without complaining that a nickel was too much. Hopefully Drift and Eva saved so much money by never wasting any on me. I remembered Dad's kaleidoscope collection, his prisms and balance beam toys. The balance beam toys were on the ledge before you went into the sunken living room. I also remember all the puzzles you gave me Dad. I can figure out a puzzle with help from above.

My great great-Grandma lived in a house on the property where my Grandparents lived. The house was in a gated community complete with a guard house. Home Sweet Home! She used to have a room downstairs in their old house.

Great Grandma washed all of our clothes in the laundry room. Mostly she hung our clothes up to dry because it was better to dry them with fresh air. Oh how grandma and grandpa hated it when great Grandma hung our clothes on a line. Maybe it upset them that my clothes were hanging out to dry too? I was not to go outside, but when grandma and grandpa were gone, Nana let me. She said it was good for a young boy to be outside in the fresh air.

The ranch house with an entry that had a stuffed deer or elk? In another part of the entry, a large model ship in an aquarium. Looking for wild horses. The Ford Bronco we drove around the ranch with instead of saddling up horses. Pieces of slate I chipped apart.

Mom took me to the Union Jack place again. She had me stay in the car. I listened to the radio. She stayed inside for a long time Breton House…again.

My Mom drove a Blue Chevy Impala. Blue with White seats, a center arm that hid away. Cool stuff back then. It was a beautiful car but not as beautiful as my Mom!

Dad took me to the overlook again. It was high enough up that you could see the whole city of Las Vegas. It was our favorite place.

I played a full sized string harp on Mom and Dad's wedding day. It was sitting there and no one was playing it. It was in the breezeway, an open walkway at the reception.

Performing my 'taxi driver' routine. Of course I copied it from my favorite clown, Red Skelton.

Our kitchen cabinet doors opened up and they were filled with health food. Raisins, Pineapple chunks, Dried fruits, Nuts, etc.. The kind of food Drift and Eva would never buy me because it was a waste of money. Drift and Eva spent money on booze and parties for their friends. They spent money on something that made them sick too. When they used it, they would throw up. Their car always smelled like puke. I know why.

Our car with a driver. Record player under the dashboard, window in the middle, hidden bar.

One of the brothers gave his wife a car with a big bowtie on it. This is when I wanted to be like the brothers, my dad and his brother. It was the time period of my life when I had no idea what was going on. I thought my Dad and his brother were 'my brothers'. I called Their Pop, POP! Oh how Maurice hated that! It made Grandma Charlotte laugh out loud though.

Maurice and Charlotte had a tough time explaining how we were all related. I know Nevada and Uncle Denver are brothers and that I am Nevada's son now. Back then though, I thought they were my big brothers. It sure was nice to know I had big brothers and even better to know who my real family is and always will be forever.

I wanted to wear pajama's like 'the brothers' wore, slippers like they wore, everything they wore I wanted to wear because I wanted to be like them. It happened after I first met them. I spent most of my crawling years at my Moms'. (Her parents' home where great Grandma raised me.) Now I stayed at my other grandparent's house in my uncles room. It didn't last for too long. I remember the moving truck. My sister went one way and I went another. From this point on I was a visitor at Dad's houses, or Grandma and Grandpa's houses, but never a family member. It really confused me. My own kind was getting rid of me again.

They were just trying a different way. They asked me to be patient and we would all get through this together and without any hard feelings. That was in about 1966. Now Drift and Eva were making some point in court about the rights they had to me. According to some paperwork they presented to the court, they were my legal guardians. Legal guardians, not parents.

Now I went back and forth and I was getting more confused. I did not realize my Dad's folks were making such a stand to protect me back then. I am impressed now, but back then I was very scared, confused, angry and constantly threatened by Drift; who was backed up by Eva.

Maurice filed the paternity suit to get me back. Finally I was going to be with my real family.

One of 'the brothers' had a motorcycle in the garage. I tried to kick start the motorcycle and started it! I know this led to a disaster of some sort.

I learned early on that I could mimic adults. I could mimic them because I watched them all the time. Only Nana watched me without to many incidents. No one else watched me without incidents because you were all too busy.

My favorite time was at the beach. I loved it when Mom would pack up my sister and I in the wagon with all of our beach toys and togs. Off to the beach! We took the station wagon with the rear window that went up and down. I know I got in trouble with the rear window going up and down. We brought Mom's picnic basket with the two special pockets built in for her two bottles of wine. Grandma Charlotte was right about Sherry wine. I liked the men who took care of our yard. They were nice and smiled at me when I was watching them. I always wanted to help.

SAN FRANCISCO

Trolley Cars and their wonderful bell ringing sounds.
Mom and Dad together and without parents around.
My Murphy Bed
The small version of Big Ben clock at Mom's school.
Getting Canvas big enough for Mom's painting's.
Storing things at the storage garage.
My Mother's father showing up and complaining about everything again.
Our fun together was over.
Why did Grandpa Gorilla call you those names Mom? Why did he call me those names too?
Why was Gorilla such a schmuck to you and I mom?
I sure am glad my Mom and Dad tried to get to know me in spite of the schmuck.

Wouldn't you be happy to know your parents tried to help you out and take the time to get to know you? The dark energy that kept me from remembering them started with bad decisions. The bad decisions were made for them because they were too young. Bad decisions were made by Grandpa Gorilla because he is a schmuck. Don't worry, he knows he is a Schmuck!

Both Grandma's flower gardens. How to grow them, prune them and take care of them. Funny they kept showing me how to take care of plants? They were showing me how to take care of living things. It was their way of explaining things to me. It helped me realize I need care too.

My Dad's apartment where everything was green. Poppa Son chair. Nice place. Girl in a cake. I know I was at my Dad's bachelor party before it started. The girl in the cake was nice to me before she had to start entertaining. Charlotte drove me home to sleep before the big day!

A train conductor is not the same as a conductor for an orchestra. Clearing up disinformation from a bad source. Maurice was an Orchestra conductor not a train conductor.

Grandma's parties had many beverages. She had wine, gin and a whole bar hidden in the closet. After that everyone was laughing and dancing. That is how I learned how to dance. Grandma's friends were nice to me. I hung out by the closet full of goodies or adult beverages.

I was grateful for the money tree my Dad gave me for my birthday. The gift was great. Dad took a small tree and put it in a planter. He stuck money to the branches. It was a great gift but mostly I was happy he was home and that he remembered! He gave me the Tonka toy dragline I wanted too! Wow! I am grateful for the gifts he gave me.

In memory of my Dad I gave my son Arizona a money tree for his Seventh Birthday.

Mom took me to the mailbox every time she helped me write a letter. I wanted my Dad to know I was okay. I wanted to tell him what I was doing, so he knew I was having fun. I wanted him to know that I loved him and wished he could be with us all the time.

My first Christmas that I remember was really nice. I helped very little because I was still crawling around, although I could walk. Mom's sister showed me what to eat. Divinity, Russian Tea Cakes, the cookies we made. My Mom's sister was very nice to me. Later my Mom's sister took me to movies or places. She was always nice to me. Thank you Auntie.

When my Dad came home it was a big deal. I remember running up on Dad's leg, he would grab my hands and I would do a flip! There was no pain involved. When Drift tried this, he would hurt my arms, hands and elbows. Of course I stopped doing it after that for obvious reasons.

Doing the 'Charleston' for my sister. We were playing around at Grandma and Grandpa's house. (Dad's side) Dancing with my sister.

Dad liked to wear a pair of blue jeans and a tee shirt. If he was smoking, he rolled a pack up in his short shirt sleeve.

I remember my Dad and his friend giving me a gold band. Dad called his friend my witness and Godfather, Drift and Eva took the ring away.

Who was the woman that changed her clothes between sets so fast? I was sitting backstage and she would come off stage sliding one outfit off as I walked behind the privacy room divider. As

the outfit came off they would powder her up quick and slide her next outfit back on over her head. Wow fast! She could really sing and dance to the full orchestra too. We rode in his car a little later and played pinball games at quiet little out of the way places.

I will call my Dad's friend, John Doe, because of who he is. He is no mystery to me. We rode around in his car. We stopped at more cafe's to play pin ball games. He was my Godfather. John and Dad gave me a gold ring. They just stopped in the middle of the road. We got out and walked to the front bumper. They said very nice things to me as they put the ring on my finger. They told me I was a special boy who had to grow up to fast like they had too. They said they knew I was protected. They drew the figure eight on the shoulder of the road. We took off.

My jack-in-the-boxes! Dad used to bring different ones to me. My Dad loved train sets. He spent a lot of time putting together elaborate scenes for the train to run through. Dad gave me boomerangs and told me how they worked. He said I could be a good boomerang if I wanted to be one and come home. He wanted me home with him and his family. I love my family.

Pulling the rope to make the church bells ring when my Mom and Dad were married. Thank You Great Grandma! You are the best! Better than all the rest.

I loved to show them the 'cannonball' in the pool.

Yes, I took the 'Nestea' plunge. I am still here and still alive! I fell backwards into an empty pool. It hurt a lot when I woke up.

I took a picture and did a painting of the driveway entry to the house in Wisconsin. It is the same house where I would visit my Dad and sister during the late summer and early fall of 1968. The home still has the pillars standing since 1968-69. It is the painting for Arizona in his Chapter.

Picking wild flowers with my sister. I talked to her and as always, she said very little. She told me she picked lady slippers and I let her know she had to stop because they are the state flower in Minnesota. Why didn't I just go pick them with you? I don't know? I should have just went and picked them with you. What do I know? Very little about girls.

My tiger's eye. Promising to write to my sister. She did not understand that I had no money for stamps and Drift and Eva would not give me any money, not to mention envelopes.

I am solid as the Rock of Gibraltar!

The house with the humidifier, my job was to fill it with water and keep it full of water.

My Mom and Dad showed me the key in the rock. It was a key for me to use to get in when no one was around. They told me I was welcome anytime to visit or to stay. It is fifty years after you gave me away, is there still a key in the rock?

Richard George is Maurice Kidd? Drift called him Richard George, but it was Maurice, it was my grandpa but I played along. I did what Drift wanted me to do because I would suffer physically if I did not make this choice.

My new adopted mother, Eva cheated at concentration. Concentration was a game show, we used playing cards to replicate the game show. She would ask me to look over there and when I looked away, she moved the cards around. I still beat her because I can see out of the corner of my eye. She ripped up the cards and did not play concentration with me ever again.

My sisters dollhouse, it was sparsely decorated and furnished. She was so excited to talk about it and how she was going to make it look when it was all done. I wanted to make miniature furniture for her. I still can if you want me too?

On some of my weekend visits, Dad would take me to the pier and we would fly different kites!

Many of my visits were to the ranch house north of Lake Havasu. The driveway to turn into was marked by an old army jeep. Of course I peeked. What Drift was doing to me was wrong.

I was always told to get down on the back floor of the car by my new dad, Drift. He only did it when we were on the way to visit my family. I would get down on the floor to avoid punishment, but at the same time I knew I was going to see everyone again. Mixed emotions always, what a tightrope to walk.

My Mom used to make me get down in the front seat when she was visiting her friends inside the Union Jack place and other places too. This was Breton House, the art and antique shop. She had me get down so no one would see me in the car. I listened to the radio. You could hear it better near the floor where the speaker was anyway. She never threatened me to stay down, she told me to for my own good.

Then the visits were on hold. I didn't see you all for a while during the court case. Why did the judge have Drift in his chambers with me when he asked me if I was afraid of Drift. What an ill-informed judge. I was scared to death of Drift! If I answered wrong he told me what he was going to do with me. He was going to put me back in the chair again!

My Grandpa, my Dad's Dad, met with Drift to figure out how to get me back. I remember being in front of a judge and lying to protect myself from being injured again by Drift and Eva. You do not understand how bad they were to me to make me that afraid. They were a very big mistake that led to so many other big mistakes in my life. I have made a final decision, I talk as little as is necessary about the mistakes in my life.

My court case was never closed. It is why Drift and Eva moved to Wisconsin. My family wanted me back. They were willing to settle for visitation while I healed from forgetting them. Drift and Eva were not cooperative in any way. I think this is what my Dad was telling me quite a few times. I remember now for what it is worth.

I was so mad at my Parents and their parents. They did not listen to me when I told them how bad I was being treated by Drift and Eva. Drift and Eva played this up. They told me no one was going to help me. Not your Family, Not your Dad and God is a joke so if you want his help, ask away and they laughed at me for saying those things.

I went to see my Dad again. I was still walking in my sleep. When you started to play music with the band, I told my friend that you are my Dad. She thought I was off my rocker. That was in 1983. I left and let you know how I felt Dad. I am sorry I flipped you off. Please forgive me. I was surprised, caught off guard and very ill informed at that time. I am very well informed now. Please forgive me?

I had a brief memory when I heard the news of your passing. I went into the bathroom and became emotional. I knew who just passed. I prayed that someday my sister would remember me. I prayed she would be healthy and live to meet with me again someday. I was in the bathroom for a long time because I was crying. I put myself together and we left.

For some reason I blocked everything out again until it all began again after another N.D.E. in 2001. I believe Drift and Eva could block my family out using a few key words.

I'll teach you a lesson.

The air mattress I paddled around on with my sister when we were at Lake Havasu.

Charlotte collected spoons from where I wound up. I am the Wisconsin spoon.

Parker and the chairs Eva used to tie us up in. The chairs and the punishment. Rick and Aunee Relic's daughter Ariel too. Eva just loved to punish little kids. This book is to wake people up who may still have time to help the children they gave away. We remember you because Our Father reminds us. He helps us remember you like a calf remembers his mother, it is natural to remember. Giving us away to others is a big mistake for everyone concerned.

Enough of them for now. I will throw my book at them! Now it is my turn to reverse what was done to me and I would appreciate my family behind me with this. I do live in the real world where my family couldn't even tell me my Dad died. I live in the real world where my family gave up on me. If Dad were alive he would be ashamed of how you are all continuing to treat me. Karma exists for us all, Thank God.

In Wisconsin, My Dad visited and gave me a glow football so we played catch in the dark. On another visit he gave me an orange laughing bag. Another gift was his miniature knife collection on a plaque. Dad's best gift to me was him coming around to visit. The house is still there.

Follow me, Where I go, What I do and What I know. My Dad followed me for a long time from Lake Havasu. I think my Dad was still recuperating from the accident. Echo Canyons when I replied to your calls. Drives into California. To the Redwoods. To the Coast. In Yosemite. In Denver. In the Grand Tetons. In Yellowstone. In the Dakotas and In Wisconsin. I love you

too! Because my Dad was dedicated to helping me remember him, I am dedicated to helping him know that I remembered him and that I am more than grateful for what he did for me. I will love you forever Dad. I love our family too.

Please Father, help me wake my family up. Sister never comes to visit. My only sister forgot me. Lady Slipper Kidd is her name and she is the only living person I thought would try to get in contact with me. I have little faith in you sister, very little respect for you at this point as well. Our Father died and you couldn't find it in your soul to get in touch with me? I hope you wake up. I hope you wake up and we can meet when we have time.

Thank you Dad for the great candies from other countries. Drift and Eva took them away when they found out we received a delivery from you. Oh how I loved the gifts you sent and that got through to me! So many did not get to me because Drift and Eva would disperse them amongst their family members. Even the car you bought for me. What I would do to drive that home to you. A 1978 Chevrolet Camaro Z28 with a throttle assembly that came apart 5 miles north of where I lived. Drift and Eva monkeyed with it. I fixed it. It was another dirty deal for Drift and Eva to lie about for personal gain. They sold the car you bought for me.

I still cherish the fact you sent me a car. A great gift, Thank You Dad.

Whatever happened to my pen pal? My sister? I mentioned I had no money to buy supplies or stamps. Isn't that what nice parents do for their children? It helped my sister give up on me because she thought I didn't want to write. I wrote messages and put the messages in bottles. I threw the bottles in the creek which flowed to the river. The river could float the message home to you. So you could save me. I gave up on anyone saving me a long time ago. The last bottle I put a message in was thrown in the creek again around 1977. I tried balloons too. No reply.

I think this book will let you all know how I feel about you, now that I am not walking in my sleep anymore. It helped to stand up to Drift and Eva. It helped to protect my son Arizona.

My kindergarten and first grade buddy, Chuck, saw my grandparents. His eyes were so big, I asked him to come in and stop acting funny. Chuck just stood there. Charlotte had to help him move towards the house. Other kids knew too! They started giving me gifts all the time. Thank you Maurice and Charlotte, God Bless You.

Some of my classmates have come forward. Many came forward when we were younger. Some of the parents of my classmates said things to me when I was younger. It is the greatest feeling in the world to know you are correct about what others have laughed at you for. I lived these memories, I forgot the times with my family because of inconsiderate and abusive foster parents. God Bless my friends and your parents who came forward. Thank You Very Much.

I found out about the paternity suit as well. It was not filed in Lake Havasu Arizona or in Las Vegas Nevada either as some had expected. Instead, I started looking around Wisconsin. There is a good chance we will find it in the same county as where my adoptive birth certificate was located. They have one certificate put in place of another birth certificate when you are adopted.

This is where the paternity suit should be found.

I went to another Elementary School in the Lake Havasu area. We lived on the corner of Park Street and Lake Shore Drive or something like that right on the lake. Only the kids across the street saw my Dad.

Some of the girls in my next new Elementary School around Havasu stopped by our apartment and wanted to play tennis with me. No one wanted to play tennis with me before my Dad showed up to visit. However, after my Dad showed up to visit me, girls began inviting me to their birthday parties. Other girls never stopped calling. One of our next door neighbors kept 'play acting' after he knocked on our door. I would open it up and he would act out a scene from Shakespeare. His name is Randolph Stetson. Thank you Randolph. Good job of acting.

The Bachelor kept me safe, I am pretty sure my Dad hired him to play catch with me and to keep me safe. Drift and Eva cut off the phone and we moved. The bachelor played chess with me. The bachelor let me drive his car. He said it was a great way to build trust. The bachelor taught me about bagels and some other traditions. God Bless You Bachelor.

Another Town in Wisconsin. Lots of kids asked me if I remembered Nevada in This Town Wisconsin. Dad talked to some of them. I knew this because they wanted me to answer questions he had for me to answer. I wish I could have answered them for you! I feel bad for forgetting all of you, but my body made the choice to protect itself from damage.

God Bless each one of you for remembering.

Lana in This Town Wisconsin knew and got in Eva's face about it. Her friend Daniella saw me with my Dad when she was at Lord Fletcher's apartments. Her dad was my football coach. His name was Mr. Anderson, a common name in Wisconsin. My Dad drove around This Town with a motorcycle helmet on, just like he did when I was younger! Dad rented a place up the hill from where we lived. He listened to ELO and other bands too. Dad smoked cigs and watched me when he had time. I know some other kids names like Jack Johnson and his friend who wanted me in their band just before we moved. They were high school seniors. God Bless each one of you for remembering.

When my Dad showed up the attention never stopped until we moved again.

JJ knew and she introduced me to some people who knew me when I lived in their neighborhood. I think a lot more people knew and said nothing to me in This Town. Jack, Dane and their sister knew. Jean's older brother knew too!

My real Grandmothers visited me in This Town. My Dad visited me in This Town. God Bless anyone in my family who visited or visits me.

One morning I came out of the bathroom and sat down at the dinner table. Jean Weber was over visiting, she was a neighbor. Jean answered to Eva, "James Garner". "Nope", Eva answered back. Jean guessed a bunch of names and Eva answered no to each one of them. Each name carried celebrity status. I later understood that she was trying to guess who my Dad was after Eva peeked her interest. This was in This Town Wisconsin. It was winter 1980. When Drift found this out he busted a chair over Eva's body. I did not help her, she never helped me.

Chicago my ex-wife, introduced me to her friends Fontaine and Bette. Fontaine asked me if anyone ever told me that I looked a lot like Nevada Kidd. I think she and my ex-wife Chicago knew what the answer was because Fontaine retracted her guess and used some other big name as her guess. Of course Fontaine recanted after Chicago took her far enough away to tell her not to mention Nevada Kidd to me. At the time, neither name mattered to me, what bothered me is that Chicago and Fontaine left me with their friend Sandy for about an hour and a half. I just met Sandy at that time and we made the best of it, but it was uncomfortable for both of us. Why would anyone care if I looked like Nevada Kidd, or Kidd K or A or whatever for that matter.

Interestingly enough we were walking around Lake Charlotte in 1987. I think I am being kind on guessing on the one and a half hours of time it took Chicago and Fontaine to discuss something I didn't recall at the time. I was still walking in my sleep. I remember now and think it is ridiculous to have even been there with them. Unbelievers are difficult to be with.

Dana Village wanted to know if I knew I looked like Nevada Kidd? She talked about it when I was working with her in Florist's warehouse. This was circa 1983 between Thanksgiving and Christmas time. We worked on Christmas trees so they were ready to be flocked. Even though I

had just watched my Dad perform that summer I had blocked him out again. Spike, Dana's friend also made a point to tell me she knew I was related to Maurice and Charlotte through some of her friends. Spike explained to me that some of the kids from my school later went to her school. Other people at the Florist's knew who my Dad was, like Lyle and Stan Baker. I just got this memory. God Bless the people at Bakerman's for trying to help me out.

Western Union Telegrams were delivered to all of my addresses in Arizona and Wisconsin.

I never got to read even one of them and I know they were all for me.

I never got to read any of my Pen Pal's letters. My Pen Pal is my sister.

We received your 'Nude' but tastefully done Christmas Card. Thank You! Wish I knew then what I know now. Drift and Eva had a fit over that card. As if Eva even resembles being a decent human being.

We always received rum cakes. I never got them either.

Drift and Eva had no TV for us to watch until 1967. Yet I watched TV with a remote control at some of the houses I visited. I even watched color TV's, which Drift and Eva never owned.

I watched 'The Green Hornet', 'Jack LaLane', 'Captain Kangaroo', 'Kukla Fran and Ollie', 'Hobo Kelly', 'Flipper', 'Sea Hunt', 'David and Goliath', 'The Flintstones'.

Do you hear me coming back home to say hello to you? I have to thank Our Father for doing this for me, Thank You Father for saying hello to everyone in my family. Thank You for helping me get my memories back, for controlling my anger over the situation, for letting me keep my memories, for keeping me alive through all the situations I had to go through to get back to you. I could Thank Our Father for everything but I think he knows how Thankful we all are in reality. He just likes to hear it, like we do. Thank You, Thank You, Thank You!

Children are property and have no rights.

I remember taking my Mom's canvasses and making a sandwich board. I took my scooter down to the fountain where I had to tell people about the end of what we know as the world.

I handed out umbrellas from one of my Grandparents homes. They had a bunch of them and the people outside didn't have any umbrellas. I knew it was going to rain. I had to convince them they would need the umbrellas later when they came home. Everyone brought them back the next day since it was raining in the evening when they came home. I told Maurice and Charlotte it would be okay because they were worried the umbrellas were gone forever. I told them each and every one would bring the umbrellas back. They learned to believe me.

Every single person brought back the umbrellas.

Dad came by in a nice Jaguar. He gave me a ride down the main boulevard and I started crying after he begged me to come home. He said he would get me new clothes and a nice bedroom of my own. Dad said, "Whatever they have done to you, we can help you, please come home?" I broke down and cried because I wanted to go home with you. I knew what would happen after that too. I was afraid of going along with you and going home with you, but not because of you Dad. I didn't go home with you because I knew the county or state would intervene and place me back with Drift and Eva. Drift and Eva made me pay for going along with you. I remember some other times when you came by and I did go home with you only to get stuck going back to the them. Please forgive me.

I remember the good and I try to erase the bad. I remember my Dad in a dune buggy with sister along. I remember when you enrolled me in the sailing club. God Bless You Dad and your patience too! I don't know how to Thank You for trying so hard and for so long to wake me up. Thank You Dad. I am trying to get back in touch with Mom and Sister and hopefully everyone else. It is nice to buy presents for your family. I know with your help I will get in touch with everyone. I will try just as hard as you did to wake me up, to wake them up. Forever!

I hope everyone likes my presence.

It has been fourteen years since I first began to remember all of you. I went to the Nevada website thinking I could get some help from the right people there. One person tried and I believe she understood my story and had heard of it before. God Bless You Juliette.

I waited because I know my family is in no hurry to contact me now that Dad is gone. They didn't even give me so much as a postcard, phone call or telegram when Dad passed in 1985. Bastard or not, that was unnecessary. How do you think I felt seeing it on TV at a New Year's Party with my new girlfriend and her family, people who had no idea why I was so emotional.

Not one of my family members has come forward since our Dad passed. It is 2015, so I will come forward. King's pawn to King's Pawn Four. I played chess with Dad too. I beat a chess-master who played sixteen games at a time and won each one. Our Dad was good at chess, I am, and Arizona is to. Did Dad play chess with any of you?

I felt sad for a long time and wished the best for my sister. I knew she was getting ill and I wished she would stay alive until after I had remembered her and we had time to meet here again before we go home. Then I blocked them out again. Back then I had no way of reaching any of you, except in my mind.

During 9-11-2001, I prayed that you would all be safe until we met again shortly. I am writing this on 3-21-2015. I hope it is obvious that I am not going to stop trying to contact you since Dad kept in touch for so long without an answer. He has the answer now though. Our Father above helped our Father just like he helps us. All the time. It is nice how things work out, although waiting to meet with you all for almost fifty years is a little long, don't you think almost fifty years is a little long to wait to be with your family again?

CORRECTING THE RECORD

There are many reasons why I have decided to go forward with my story. The first reason is to verify to Our Father that his work exists and always has for me through my trials and tribulations. Have you seen the light? In the light there are many things possible, all of which I do not understand and all that I am thankful for as well as all the deeds he has done for me. My belief alone in Our

Father who created us all, has saved my life many times without me even understanding why, until now. Thank You Father.

The second reason is for my own mental health. I finally have the ability to think of myself as an important entity, a person with a background to be proud of no matter what human mistakes were made. "I am Somebody", I am what I am. Isn't it slightly easier when you have a living example that resembles you in like looks, thoughts and beliefs? Someone who cares about you?

Thirdly I Thank my son Arizona. Standing up to the two people who scared me into denying my own parents was so freeing! Lucky for them I did not take care of business the way I wish I could have taken care of business. By standing up to them for trying to hurt Arizona made me scared, nervous, anxious, but I stood up to them without thinking of myself. My only concern was to protect my only son Arizona. They left when I told them to pack their stuff up and get out!

After that I am thanking my friends for believing in me. Thank You to all my childhood friends, some of whom I have mentioned previously and to all of the rest. Thank You!

I thank my new best friend Faith Keeper. She is my girlfriend and companion in all things.

I am now thanking anyone who believes in me. It sure feels good.

The Thanking Chapter, that's what I will call this part of the book.

If you have a thanking chapter you have to have a giving chapter. I hope I can give my family, friends and anyone who believes in Our Father the same good things that have come to me through the Father. I have a saying now, "The more you give, the more you get to give". Try it, it is true! If it is really hard to give anything material, give of yourself. It is the promise I made to Our Father. I have to serve him when he calls. Since we have free will, it is hard to do this here, but I have reacted to situations without thinking and later thought about why I just did and it causes me to realize he is in us all the time.

It also feels really good when I think about who gave me the intuition to react and get things done. I believe it was my Fore Fathers and Fore Mothers. God Bless All Of You.

At a very busy intersection, a car was headed for pedestrians after the guy driving got out of the car. He left it running and in gear! I jumped out of my car and headfirst into the window of the moving car. I pushed the clutch in with my hand and the brake with my other hand, the car stopped. I took the car out of gear. I turned the key off and got back out of the now, not moving car and jumped back into my car. An acquaintance that was with me asked, "What did you do that for?" I answered, "I don't know, someone had to do something".

I was a school crossing guard when I went to school. When I was on the south side of the busy boulevard on the corner. I pulled a kid out of the way of a car that went through my flag. I don't know their name, but they know their names.

I sure have a lot of memories for this to be a figment of my imagination. I do not like it when people call my story a hoax or false. It used to affect me knowing what kind of Karma was in front of me. I know what to do now, leave them to Our Father in Heaven.

Now I should be able to get in communication with my family. There is the internet, my memories and my intuition to help me connect the dots. That is another reason why I am writing this all down.

I am in to making new memories! I am into reconnecting with my real family now that I have disconnected from my fake family. What my fake family did to me would not have been possible had my real family decided to keep me instead of giving me away. Due to my Mother's age, it was not her decision to make, so I have no malice towards my Mother. My Father made some mistakes as Mom did, but he too was not part of the decision. Please remember, my Father visited me from 1965 through 1985. My Mom and Dad loved each other when they made me. Both my Mom and Dad told me that when I was a boy. It is all I needed to know.

I have to say something at this point. I received my memories through near death experiences in which I was saved 'miraculously' over and over until I remembered for good and wrote it down. I know who can intervene and change the outcome of what should have certainly meant injury at the very least. Yet I walked away over and over until I remembered for good and wrote it down.

My Grandpa Maurice was ill and visiting me in 1968, he said nicer things to me. I forgave him. God Bless You Maurice. I know how hard you tried to make things right. Thank You.

Before 1968, Maurice got Drift a cup of coffee and a cocoa for me. They sat down and told me to, "Go get busy, head out there". They shut the door behind me after scooting me out of the room. The office girls were nice to me. They were doing all of my Dad's mail for him. My Dad got bags and bags of mail to be looked at every day. No wonder it took him a while to write back to me. The letters came to the girls, they told me it was nice to finally meet the little boy that wrote to his Dad. Oh if I could find one of those fan club girls. Oh if I could find my letters that I wrote to you.

The girls would tell me nice stories. They would get me more cocoa. They thought it was nice that I could read and write already. They were not bank tellers like Maurice and Drift wanted me to believe. Maurice Kidd was my grandfather. I went along with the gag when Drift called him Bill or George or whatever..

Then it was time to leave. Sometimes I would go back with Drift right away. Other times I was picked up by Mom, or Dad, or Mom and Dad. That is when I spent time with my Mom and Dad. Sometimes Grandpa Maurice would take me home with him to visit Grandma.

Anyone wondering how I got this straight and why it took so long?

The best times were when I was able to see my great Grandma and my Sister. We always had fun together. After Nana gave us our choice of cones and ice cream, she showed us the pedal car our uncle put together or fixed up. It was in the garage near the road away from the house. Our uncle put blocks on the pedals to make it easier for my short legs! She opened up the garage doors and we rolled it out and I pedaled it around the neighborhood.

That was the house where the guard at the guard shack let you in and out. It had big trees in the yard and it was the house I was raised in to start my life. My sister and I sat in the pedal car and I steered and pedaled. She went and did something else, but I kept pedaling around the streets in our gated community in the pedal car. It was so great to be back again! In a gated community, there is no traffic! I could drive around without any danger. Great Grandma made ice cream cones, our choice of cone. I was playing with my sister. The best memories.

I wonder if my Sister remembers going swimming, snorkeling, looking at anything under water.

The business of getting rid of me was complex, because I remembered them and they

remembered me. My Dad remembered me and tried so hard and for so long to get me to remember. I remember now! My whole family on my Dad's side tried to get me to remember. God Bless them.

Prayers are answered. Talking to Our Father in Heaven is a daily thing. I know he talks to everyone. There are many events in my life that are extremely significant to me. The most important thing is that I know who saves me when I get into trouble. He does it instantly.

Why?

So I could remember who I am? So I could share this story? It is his plan and I would never dream of interfering with Our Father's plan. I will give him my helping hands.

Thank You Father in Heaven and to my real Parents, my Son, my real Grandparents, all real fathers and mothers before, real uncles and aunts, real cousins and friends and neighbors.

Thank You

Make a good show.

CHAPTER TWO

For My Son, Arizona

You have heard this story a few times and I am almost certain you have had your doubts. I have even had mine before I became healthy again. You have to know that you were the catalyst behind all of this Z. If you remember, I told you there was a brother of yours out there and that your Mom was angry at first when I told you. I think my prayers were answered again because your Mom decided to search for him. Your Mom found him and it was a little tough at first, but everyone was better for it.

Now you know your brother Steve! Your Mom knows her other son now too.

This story is for you and is mostly about you. I had to show you and tell you what I could before I have to go. Once I am gone it will be difficult to search for our real family. If my real Dad was alive, it would have been simple. He is gone Arizona. He is still a loyal, caring and understanding Dad who was put through hell because of others making bad decisions for him. He made a bad decision too, but he did love my Mom and he married her. They met and were in love from before high school. My Mom was under age when they were expecting me. She was still underage when I was three years old. I believe twenty one years old was the legal age back then. Mom was born in 1945 and I was born in 1961, you can do the math. This was taboo in 1961. This same sort of thing altered other's artist's careers.

Mom's Dad, Gorilla McGillicudy, took me to an orphanage because he was under pressure by our wonderful 'judgmental' society. He had accumulated some good standing in society along with the earthly rewards as well. He is a human being and he did what many human beings did back then and now, he rid himself of what he thought was a threat to his good standing. Need I tell you how I felt.

My other Grandfather was in agreement at first. He too was in good standing with our judgmental society. He and my other Grandfather worked together through my elimination process. When I figured this out, I was really angry. I hung myself so they could get off easy. Gorilla, my Mom's Dad stuck to his guns, but my other grandfather turned to try and help me. My paternal side was loyal to me, but not in a way you might think right away. In spite of all this Arizona, my Dad came to visit and he brought his brother and father.

We talked and played music together.

We played crazy 8's! They taught me how to say, "Go Fish!"

I rode on my Dad's back when he played pretend horsey!

They brought me Jack-In-The-Boxes! They brought me gifts, they remembered me.

Arizona, they changed their bad decision to a good one.

However the story has taken a turn for the very worst. Now Drift and Eva have entered the arena and they are going to give all of us trouble from that point until I remembered everyone in 2001. I take that back, they did testify against me to take you away from me in 2002. Did you know that? They sided with your mom to take away my rights as your father. Nice people huh? Drift, Eva and their son each wrote and signed an affidavit against me. Your mom took the court documents accusing me of being a crack user to the little league, soccer association and the basketball association.

I was never allowed to coach again thanks to your mother and her allegations.

The judge heard both sides and asked your mothers lawyer if she could define 'juris prudence'? She asked her where she studied law?

The judge asked her if she understood that she could not judge against me because and I quote, "I cannot make a decision based on what he said, she said and what they said". She let your mom's lawyer know she needed evidence to support that I was a danger to my son. She had no evidence Arizona because I do not do crack! I do not even drink very often. I don't like to drink and do drugs. I also happen to love you and I would never hurt you. I didn't even spank you. After reading this maybe you understand why I would never hit you. Your mom should have known better, a sign she was making poor decisions. It is what happens when you make poor decisions. Her poor decisions marked an end to my having any chance of ever trusting her again.

The judge asked these simple questions because I didn't even have a parking ticket on my record. I have some blemishes Arizona but none are anything I am worried about when I see Our Father in Heaven. Even though the allegations were destructive and damning, I forgive your mother. I never forget though.

When you were still a baby in your crib, I told you that someone is watching and protecting you. It felt funny at the time, but I knew it was the truth. I was still in my walking sleep. I know you talk to Our Father in Heaven all the time, because it is something we have inside of us. He helped me through all my life and continues to do so.

When you were very little, I stayed home and took care of you. Your mother was not happy I wasn't working. I was in a head-on car accident at 50 mph. Thought I had better mention that fact. I was laid up for a long time.

You were a very healthy baby boy who was also in need of attention. The first thing your Mother and I noticed was that you did not want to miss anything. You did not go down for your nap very well and you were even worse at bedtime. I had to drive you around in the car to get you to go to sleep. Dad used to do the same thing for me when he was home.

It reminded me of how I was when I was young.

You were so easy going and easy to take care of once I understood what you wanted. When you were little we put VHS tapes into the video player and you watched children's stories. I told you other stories about whatever you were interested in. It was the greatest thing I had ever done. I learned how to take care of you, but it wasn't because of Drift and Eva that I taught you good things. It was because I was beginning to remember another family, but I could not connect my memories back then. I remember teaching you that the truth is all around you, not in a book.

Mostly you liked it when I played music. Since I loved music, we played it all the time. One time you crawled over and turned the stereo up real loud. I came over, turned it down, heard you screaming, picked you up, turned the music off and held you to make sure you knew you were okay.

When I held you, I remembered how someone used to do that for me before Drift and Eva. Drift and Eva never held me to comfort me ever. My real family did comfort me Arizona.

When you came into the world, your Mom and I loved you and we always will.

That is what was missing with my upbringing. At first my upbringing was pretty normal. I was being raised by my great Grandmother. Great grandmother's teapot would whistle and wake the whole house up! My family loved me and cared about me. My Nana tucked me in at night but others did too, even my reluctant Grandpa, Grandma and great Grandma gave him a look, it worked. Thank you to my whole family for all you have done and are about to do again.

Mom and her sibling's fought over the upstairs bathroom. When I came along and was starting 'potty training', I created a large problem with one more person for the bathroom. Grandpa talked with me about how long I spent in the bathroom and that others needed it like I need it.

Grandpa Gorilla was firm with me, but never mean like my foster parents Drift and Eva. He did let me stay alive and under his roof when I was little. I felt safe with my mom's family.

My Mom, her younger sister and brother went to school. One by one they went in the bathroom; day after day and all while I 'held it' in my bedroom next to the bathroom. I learned if you didn't get up, you didn't have to go as bad.

Nana always had a nice breakfast. She was not very happy when someone did not stop to eat or not have enough time to eat. My Mom was the worst of the bunch. I liked breakfast a lot, Nana made the best breakfast, lunch and dinner! She prepared our food with love.

Everyone would come downstairs one by one and sit down to breakfast. Except my Grandma, she had a mind of her own. Almost as soon as breakfast started it was finished. Uncle was off to school with his friends and so was my Mom and her sister. Grandma went back upstairs if she came downstairs at all or to the "sunroom".

Grandpa went to work every day and was home at five o'clock sharp. He was always gone for weekend's for his work somewhere. He was into a 'routine'. That is what he demanded, that we stick to his routine. Grandpa made his decisions and stuck to his decisions good or bad. He was a soldier and a pilot. Our Father in Heaven could depend on Gorilla to get things done.

Great Grandma looked at me and I looked at her. She cleaned me up after eating and changed me. Then she took me downstairs to the playroom with two rocking horses in the corner. I always wanted to ride the rocking horses, but I couldn't walk yet.

I played with my Barn Set. To play with it, you opened up the barn roof and pulled out fencing, animals, water troughs, everything for a farm! I played with dominoes a lot too. My great Grandma 'showed me'. My uncle had toys, but he only shared his old 'baby' toys with me. He 'showed me' too. Everyone was into showing me things when I was very little. They were really into showing me their goofy faces. Wish I could show you what you looked like.

Do you remember me making 'goofy faces' Arizona? When you see the bright white light, you might. We are in good hands. All you have to do is believe and make good decisions, correct the bad ones. You have the ability to do this with ease. Our Father gives us signs. He helps us.

My great Grandma went upstairs and did laundry, or dishes, or cleaned the house. She liked to take care of us because she loved us all. Nana let me get the mail and the newspaper when I could walk. I would bring it to the desk with a phone on it near the kitchen.

I would help my great Grandma with whatever she needed help with every day. I helped her with the dishes, the laundry, I hummed to the vacuum and she laughed.

I loved my Family too, just like I love you Arizona. I love Our Father in Heaven for giving me back my memories and I was so happy I cried. What would I be able to tell you about them if he had not intervened? What would I be able to tell you if my father and his father had never visited me? We are a family, all of us at home and down here, no matter where we are, we are family and we love each other. Let me share some more and show you what I mean.

Even Grandma came down for lunch. Sometimes she made lunch, but usually great Grandma made lunch. After lunch was time for me to get changed and take a nap.

I hated naps. You hated naps too Arizona.

I usually woke up before Grandpa got home from work. When Grandpa was about to come home, I would be excited. Great Grandma would help me get the mail and the newspaper to him. When I was a little older I pushed the ottoman under his shoeless feet. I loved my Grandpa. He loved me too. He thanked me when I did these things. He would say, "Thank You Kid, now run along and see if they need help in the kitchen." He was a private man.

Supper was on shortly after Grandpa was home from work. He liked it when he could smell it cooking and it was his favorite! His favorite dish was the one in front of him! Great Grandma always had me set an extra plate for the stranger. A plate, silverware on a napkin and a glass. I asked my great Grandma if we could skip setting the table for the stranger because he never comes.

Great Grandma let me know that we had to be ready for the stranger to visit at any time and that the extra place setting for him would make him feel more comfortable. It made sense to me. Great Grandma was the only one at the table who made sense to me.

As I grew, I began to understand I was not the most welcome of surprises to my family. The bachelor came by to pick up my Mom. Sometimes it was my Dad and sometimes it was other bachelor's. One time I caught one of her other bachelors in her bedroom. I had a bad dream and woke them up, I wanted to be with my Mom when I was afraid. I know who he is, JoJo took me to my school, he took me to get tacos and to just drive around. JoJo wrote a song for my Mom, my Dad and me. I cannot prove he did, but I know the story and I know JoJo.

I was not spying on anyone. I had a bad dream and wanted my Mom. My Mom wouldn't come to the door. She told me to go to my room and wait. I was afraid to go to my room, that's where I had the bad dream. So I told my Mom I was going to get Nana. I knocked on the door and still no response, so I looked in the keyhole and saw someone besides Dad with my Mom. Now I was mad and had to get in the room. I went to get Nana and her door opened.

That is how I met JoJo, Mom's friend.

One time I brought my Mom breakfast in bed and she was happy.

One time I brought my Mom breakfast in bed and she threw it off the bed and yelled at me for making a mess and waking her up. I never made my Mom breakfast in bed again. No Mimosa's either.

My Mom can cut her own birthday cake.

I used to get cigarettes and beer for my Dad and his friend Top. Top worked on wood boats. We would visit him and sit up on the boat. I was the runner to get them what they wanted.

"Hey Kid" could you run in the house and get us some beers. I was happy to do this for them.

Off I went to get them some beers in the house. Down the ladder, run to the door, go in and open up the fridge door, shut it, run back out and climb the ladder and hand them the beers. I would hand them tools, cigs, and I would hold the light for them. I wanted to help my Dad because I love him. They thanked me for what I did for them. They were grateful.

Another day when we were visiting, they misplaced their cigs.

"Hey Kid," could you find us our cigs. "Sure thing," and I was looking around the boat as fast as I could to find their cigs right away. I found them by the captain's chair after a few minutes.

"Here they are," I said. "Okay," hand them to us with the matches. "Which ones?" I asked.

What do you mean which ones? I answered, "There are cigs inside the pack and there are cigs that look different in between the outside of the pack and the wrapper."

"Hand us the pack kid" and they laughed. Dad and Top had fun together back then. My Dad had a friend in Wisconsin too. Bob lived in the same gated community at the time. He and Dad would talk for a while and sister and I would run around the woods. My Dad was recovering from the accident still. I still feel bad about that accident. I wish he wasn't hurt.

This is probably all nonsense to you for the first time or so reading this, but in time, I believe you will understand it all just like I understand.

I'm sorry your Mom and I couldn't get along. She doesn't believe me like you do. She should know I mean what I say.

One thing I learned early on about you is your ability to focus or concentrate. When you liked something, you could figure out a way to get it pretty easily. I was good at that too.

Now to get down to business. If there is anything you want to know about your childhood, call me, I would be glad to share it with you. One story in particular Arizona is very significant to me.

Drift and Eva were visiting in 2000 at our house. We were all talking when you walked in the living room and waited near me. I knew you had to tell me something, but you were waiting to tell me when you had a chance. Five minutes passed and there was a break in conversation. I took you to the side to ask you what you needed. You tried talking to me and Eva threw a fit. She intervened as though you were interrupted everything and you needed scolding. You needed no scolding Z.

Eva stood up yelling at how rude you were to interrupt, and then she grabbed you and dragged you into your bedroom. I was in shock, but no one was going to treat you like they treated me.

I followed very closely behind and unbeknownst to Eva. She was so into, Teaching you a lesson." Eva threw you on your bed and raised her hand. I opened the door to this and told her to get away from you. She told me to mind my own business!

Arizona, you are my business! I think by now you know we can take care of business.

I told her to get away or I would help her learn how to regret even thinking of what she was going to do to you. Eva would not back down. Again she told me to get out of her way so she could and I quote her, "I'm going to teach this little brat a lesson". This pissed me off!

Now she struck a chord in me.

She talked like that to me all the time when I was young. Eva hit me, grabbed and pulled my arm with no regard as to how much it hurt from three years old on. She was not going to do the same things to you Z!

She kicked me, slapped me and tied me to a chair and laughed at me from three years old on. It was all I could do not to flatten her for treating you this way.

I remembered how she and Drift treated me. They never loved or cared about me, ever.

So I told her and Drift to get their belonging's packed up and get the hell out of my house! She got the message and left. I will be forever grateful that I stood up for you when no one else stood up for me against those two PIGS! I never felt better because I knew you were my boy! You are absolutely worth standing up for Arizona and I will do it for you every time.

You are the only family I have that believes in me. I am grateful I have friends that believe in me, but it means a whole lot more coming from you!

You will figure out who we are related too. Maybe you remember who I told you we are related too? I think you remember.

This chapter is for you to know how Thankful I am, that you are my Son.

Through you Arizona, I was able to remember how my bad parents treated me. By seeing how ludicrous it was that they over-reacted to what you did, and you did nothing wrong Arizona. It was beyond obvious that they were trying to do the same things to you. We will not talk about them ever again after I write the chapter for unbelievers. I hope you like everything I am writing.

Most of it is for you Arizona. The rest of my family stopped looking for me. Here is hoping!

I love Our Father in heaven for everything he showed me so I could share it with you. He showed me my memories of me with my real family. Many people will doubt this story, it is okay, they doubt everything anyway. That is what happens to people who lack faith and the ability to believe in Our Father in Heaven.

You see, if you believe in the Father, he believes in you.

Make a good show.

CHAPTER THREE

For Future Kidd's and what you can share with them

This chapter is for your children Arizona. Even before you see them, you will love and care about your children. I loved you the moment we found out.

Our Father shows us all the time how much he loves and cares about us. He shows us so that we know right from wrong.

Of course we have free will.

Free will gives us the chance to make our own decisions, sometimes good, sometimes bad.

Our Father gave us free will so we could learn what it is like to feel everything good and bad. So we could learn how to listen to what is inside us and make our own decisions.

When we talk with him directly you know he is guiding us towards the good and away from the bad. You will get signs constantly and just in time, it is amazing what he does for us.

It is hard for us to understand what his plan is for us, but it sure is clear that he can help us if we let him. Just ask and wait, when you least expect it, the answer will be right in front of you and obvious who you received the answer from.

When I was little, I talked with him all the time. He is always around. He sees everything we see, because he sees everything through our eyes. That is how he knows what we are doing. That is how he can record the memory. That is how he shows us our life when we are near him.

Even little children know why he is around all the time. Who helps us forget?

The unbelievers. Watch out for the unbelievers. They are here to do bad things.

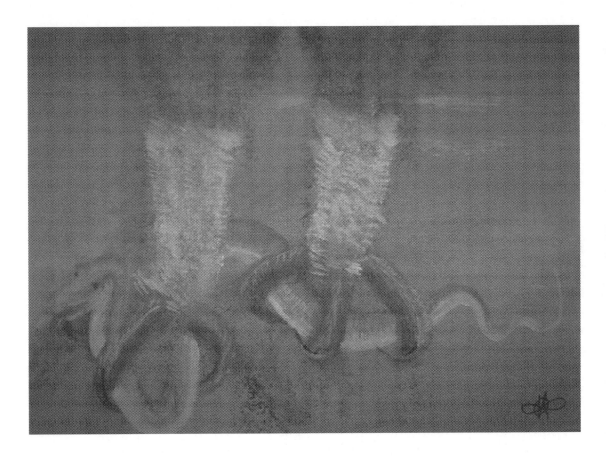

CHAPTER FOUR

For Unbelievers

I am clear about the orphanage loaning me out to a few couples to try me out for a weekend.

I am surprised they didn't kick my tires and look under my hood first. I was such a thing.

When I was adopted, I was just property and not as important as a car or a house. I was an extra mouth to feed, something on top of everything else to take care of. I've heard it all!

The last couple chose me but not my older friend who protected me at the orphanage. He wanted to go with me as my 'brother', but he could not and I could not help him. I wished I could, do you remember? Thank you for protecting me. You are a shining example of how someone could be so mistreated and still offer to help a brother. Really we are all brothers and sisters.

From that point on I thought of you as my brother. God Bless You Brother for offering to help me. I am trying to help children like us now. I may be late, but I have a story to share and change how they think about children. We should never be allowed to be treated like property!

I wanted to start this chapter out with a good story amongst so many bad stories. I believe it is good to write the truth, be it good or bad, and it is about time I told the truth about the worst people in my life, the unbelievers.

There is really very little room to write about the two worst people I have ever known and never want to see.

I am leaving the worst people in my life in the hands of Our Father in Heaven.

I will be relieved when I am done with this chapter.

In order to move forward, I must rid myself of what was done to me and others. At first I was going to really give it to the ones who mistreated me for so long and to everyone in their family and friends. That would be playing into the hands of the dark side of life. So I have decided to write down the comparisons of good and bad as I witnessed.

First memories in order, playing musical chairs, wearing a school uniform, my lunchbox, raincoat and boots, no lunch and writing on the chalkboard punishment for playing the musical chairs game, out the window and these memories led to my great Grandmother, Nana!

I compared my first memories and the people with Drift and Eva. Drift and Eva did not re-enroll me in my private school because it was too expensive. They put a peanut butter sandwich in a brown paper bag for my lunch when they remembered. They gave my raincoat away, gave away my boots, gave away my hat, and gave me no love, no caring and absolutely no compassion as to how someone should treat a three or four year old. They gave away my gifts from my family, to their family and friends or worse. They pawned the gifts you gave me Dad.

My real name is Gorilla after Mom's dad. Drift and Eva didn't like my real name. They kept punishing me until I took my new dad's name, Drift. They took it to extremes when they tied me to a chair. They tied my feet, they tied my hands, they tied my arms, they tied my body to the chair so good I could barely breathe. When I would not stop talking and yelling for help, they gagged me so I could not scream and then ungagged me when I promised to be good and do what they told me.

They would torture me by not giving me any water for a long time, nor any food. When they did give me water, they threw it at my face, or poured it on my head. They would heat a fireplace poker end up to red hot and put it in my face! They did this and laughed while they were doing it to me. This is only the tip of the iceberg and could easily be another book or more, but why share a story that is full of horror, violence and pure hatred for me and my real family.

Drift and Eva thoroughly enjoyed what they were doing!

I thoroughly enjoy what am writing about now, because it gives Drift and Eva back everything they gave to me, including this bullshit name they stuck me with!

My name is Gorilla Kidd!

I cried out for my Mother and Father to help me out of this place!

I cried out to my Fathers Father's and to my Mother's Mothers before them.

PLEASE HELP ME!

No one came except Our Father. I have been in his hands ever since and always have been. He is bright, as in so bright that you know it is him. I took the name I have now and lived out my life in a walking sleep. I have been protected since the beginning of time and will always be protected because I believe in our God, the Father!

All of us can do this! It is easy to believe.

I am sharing this in the unbelievers chapter because they think my story is a joke.

Unbelievers think Our Father in Heaven is a joke and that his sons and daughters are a joke.

Believers feel sorry for the unbelievers, but we cannot help you anymore. You have to help yourselves.

Oh I have tried to get through to them, but you have to draw the line somewhere. So I am writing a book to show them how they could come back and be with their Father in Heaven. There is always a path home if you are willing to start walking. You will see it is easy to be guided correctly. For anyone who wants to be guided, look for comparisons. Let me show you.

COMPARISONS

This is how I am going to proceed. I will share some of the list of my memories with you. I will go down my list one by one and show the comparisons for you to read. I will not go through every one of them, just enough to insure the reader I know the differences now. When you know the differences, you can make the right choice and continue further on the path.

My Mother drove my Sister and I around to the beach, the store, the doctor and many other places. Eva did not have a driver's license until 1981 and never drove me anywhere. Only Drift drove us around. This comparison should have been easy for me to logically know the difference. At the time though, when I was three, I did what I was told to avoid more pain. Our Father in heaven asked me to trust him through all of this. I trust him still.

My real Dad loved me and liked when I called him 'Daddy'! I was three years old! Drift punished me and told me I was a baby when I called him 'Daddy'. He wanted me to call him Father or Dad. Can you imagine being punished for calling your father Daddy?

That boils my blood to think about that, I bet my real Daddy's blood is boiling too. I was three!

My mother would scold me if I did something wrong. When I did something wrong in my new house, Eva would slap me, spank me, and she yelled at me all the time! Eva even tied up Mike, supposedly their son and a girl I called Ariel.

Ariel is Carlos and Carmalita's daughter. Eva was babysitting for Carlos and Carmalita. Ariel broke an etch-a-sketch over my head. Eva grabbed Ariel by her neck from behind and even though Ariel was kicking and screaming, Eva was grinning telling her what she was going to do to her. Remember Eva? Remember what Eva likes to say?

"I'm going to teach you a lesson," Eva said it all the time. That is what she told Ariel and everybody else. I sure hope you like what all your lessons will add up to for you Drift and Eva.

Drift and Eva, please listen carefully, Our Father in Heaven has some lessons for us all and even he lets us make our own decisions!

Eva did not see Ariel's Mom drive up. Eva had Ariel all tied up to the chair in seconds. I didn't know it then, but I do now, Eva had it planned, the ties were right by the chair. Eva told me to go over to the outdoor faucet and turn it on. She was yelling at me to turn the water on. I didn't turn the water on because the hose was in the sun. The water inside the hose would have burned Ariel. Eva was so angry with me that she yelled even more at me, ran over and started hitting me and still had no idea Ariel's Mom untied Ariel and was trying to rescue her daughter. Eva was more concerned about yelling, kicking and hitting me to turn the water on. Eva was oblivious to Ariel's Mom saving her daughter and when they were running away, Eva saw them and chased them to their car threatening them.

How could I have stayed with Drift and Eva after this? Was it not clear to Carmalita that I might need a little help to get away from these two monsters? She was mad at Eva no doubt. She was happy just to get away from Eva, I never saw her, Ariel or Carlos ever again. They were not the only ones. There were plenty of people pissed off at Drift and Eva over the years.

My real Grandmothers were good to me. Drift and Eva's mothers were not nice to me at all. Eva's Mom stuck her tongue in my mouth all the time when she kissed me. Our Father in Heaven has her under control.

Both of my real Grandfathers typed in their home offices. Drift and Eva's Fathers did not work in offices. One worked in a paper factory and one was a drunk.

Mom's Dad, my Grandfather Gorilla, was a decorated veteran. A football player and in later years a writer like my other grandpa and me. After I woke up I found out that my Grandpa was really good at football, but mostly he was trying to be a decent human being. He made mistakes as we all do, I forgive him and my other Grandpa too. I understand what we are forced to do sometimes and I do not like making mistakes either. I am honored to be your First Grandson. I cannot say the same for Drift and Eva's fathers.

Mom's Mom, my Grandmother Jane, was a very pretty woman. She had a prominent make up vanity and mirror. There were perfume sprayer bottles all over the top of her vanity, make-up containers of all shapes and sizes too. My Mom would ask her for money and Grandma gave it to her. Both my Mom's and my Dad's Mothers had flower gardens. Mom's Mom had three children and Dad's Mom had two children.

Eva's Mom was not a pretty woman and neither was Drift's mom. Neither had a vanity and mirror with perfume sprayer bottles anywhere. Neither gave any money away to anyone, 'they both gave at the office'. One Grandma had a vegetable garden to feed her ten kids and the other had no garden. Eva's mom never had a garden but she did kiss her six kids.

Do you know what it is like to have Eva's mother give you a wet kiss?

My real Grandmothers would NEVER do something like this to me.

I can go on and on but it works me up to want to get back at bad people. I do not get back at anyone. It is hard to resist this temptation because of all the bad decisions made for me for so long and the punishment that went with it. I had to endure all of this while knowing no one in my family could help me. NO ONE helped me except Our Father in Heaven.

I chose to see the light of Our Father, Our God. I chose to believe in the face of great darkness. I still see the light!

How-did-I-not-notice-the-differences? I could go on and on but do not want to give too much time to the bad people in my life. They are not worth it. They do the bad things because they crave power at all costs. They are angry because they are powerless in the light!

I remember everything you did to me and Arizona remembers what you did to him as well. Lucky for the two of you I have morals and respect for humanity. You have forgiveness for what you did to me, but I will never forget what you did to me. Arizona has his own way of dealing with what you did to him. Now I have the privilege of sharing it with the world, so the world can see what a wealthy family can do in order to stay wealthy. They gave me away to anyone, without any verification of character in any way, just to be rid of me fast! I forgive Gorilla because I know he cared about me and loved me. He is my Grandfather and I am his Grandson. Somebody has to be the bad guy, it wasn't me at three years old for God's sake.

So the whole world can see what two people can do to a child in order to make a buck. I even know how much they were paid a month. $500.00 a month, which back in 1965 was quite a sum of money. Drift and Eva also received money from my family to keep my life story out of sight, out of mind and there is a word for this. Let us not forget the bonus money for Drift and Eva to buy a 1966 Ford Galaxie 500, a new travel trailer and enough money to give Eva an operation. If there is one cockroach to see, there are thousand's and possibly millions out of sight.

I wonder how much was really paid out. To the Doctor? The Hospital? The clerk at the State of Wisconsin? Oh the trail of money always leads to someone's wallet. I know who wrote the checks, it was my Dad. I saw his checks a few times. In my Dad's biography it tells of a fund for orphans. Anyone want to guess who the orphan might be?

I wonder how much Gorilla or the orphanage paid to the doctor that signed my false birth certificate in Wisconsin? It is false, why, because there is no record of my birth at the hospital listed on the certificate.

There is a birth certificate in Wisconsin that took hours for me to get. The clerk let me know that it took time since there were complications. Less than a minute after they gave it to me, they took it back and gave me the one I have now. They told me it was the wrong one and they had to give me a different one. I told them I wanted it back and they said they could have me removed by security. The same thing happened at the social security office. Anyone can look at their records with social security, but if I even try they threaten to call security again.

I went to the hospital listed on the Wisconsin Birth Certificate. They have no record of my birth. They have no record of a room for my alleged birth mother, Eva. They have no record check in or check out of the hospital for either one of us on the day I was born. This is a common problem with adoptions. One certificate is replaced with a phony.

I found out that Eva was in this hospital in August of 1961. Eva's friend who told me also shared with me that Eva was not pregnant in August of 1961. Eva's friend, Eva's sister, Eva's brother and other family members of Eva's and Drift's. I called many of their family members to tell them I found out the truth about my adoption, but only the ones I thought would share the truth with me. Some did and some did not. Thank you to the ones who shared with me. The truth will set you free. God Bless You!

TWO OLD DOGS CHANGE THEIR SPOTS AND DO NEW TRICKS

My Mother's father started to be nice to me. He let me get him the newspaper without crabbing at me. He let me light his pipe. It was strange that he was being nice to me, because up to that point, he was determined to get rid of me. He even promised me a ride if I was good. I loved to ride in cars then and I still do now. Not to mention, I was excited that grandpa had a change of heart.

Some time passed and my grandma's both spent time with me in the garden. They explained the birds and the bees, (Age appropriate for a four year old), they had tea parties with me invited, instead of shunned.

One night grandpa told me we were going for a ride the next day. For some reason, no one was home that next morning. Great Grandma made us breakfast, but everyone left the house. Grandpa let me know I had to get ready to go and he was going to start up the car. Oh boy, finally, grandpa was going to give me a ride in his car. He told me where we were going was a surprise.

He took me to the orphanage. They had to sedate me and threaten me to keep me there.

Thank you grandpa. The next time I saw you, I squared off with you and told you what I thought of you. Someone has to be the bad guy for my story to have drama! I have only good for you still Grandpa in spite of what your bad decision did to me.

I know you remember. You may be gone, but now you are not forgotten. I am taking your name back because it was given to me by my Mother, your daughter. My Mother thought you would be honored by her naming me after you. I am honored as I should be and will take it back when Our Father in Heaven decides it is the right time.

I know now why you did it, why you gave me away. I feel sorry for you. God Bless You for completing your mission. I hope I am as blessed as you are when I complete mine. Thank You Grandfather! God Bless You Gorilla.

As for my other multi-talented grandfather. My Dad's Dad, Maurice Kidd. I saw you more after my other Grandfather got rid of me than before. You were mostly kind, smiley and nice even as you did the paperwork for the paternity suit. Drift would take me to see you at your office, your home in Las Vegas, your home on Lake Havasu, your home in Lake Havasu on the hill by the airport, the courthouse, and many other places that were meeting places to drop and pick me up at and from. Maurice was such a great guy, he even invited Drift and Eva over for parties. Fondue, BBQ, deck parties. Maurice treated Drift like a king. He treated Drift like a king because you treat your enemies better than your allies. Maurice despised Drift and Eva.

At first I thought you were completing paperwork to be rid of me forever. Fortunately for all of us, we have Our Father in heaven to show me that you had another motivation. You were trying to reverse my adoption. I know about the paternity suit. I know where to look. Thanks to you for trying so hard to help me see you and our family again. God Bless You Maurice.

I think Our Father in heaven appreciates it when families get back together. I think Our Father likes it when we are happy and on the right path. It is hard to stay on the right path when so many decisions were wrong, but with his help, it became easy. I like writing this down because it is making me feel better. Thank You Father in Heaven for letting me be awake to see my family again. Thank You!

Thank You for protecting me and my family, Father. Thank you for believing in me. You were the only one for a long time. Even when I was angry at everything and even you, you still believed in me. Thank You.

I Pray that my family is awake. I pray that they will wake up if they are asleep and believe in Our Father in Heaven, in time to go home and be with family too. I only hope the best for others and that even goes for the unbelievers. I don't talk much about them anymore. Even talking about them works me up to make bad decisions.

On to good decisions.

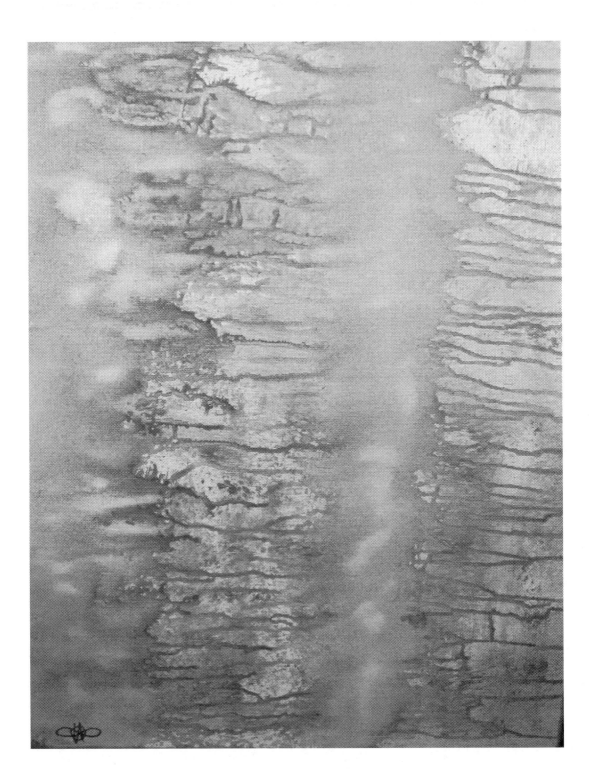

CHAPTER FIVE

Mom and Dad

Mom took me to see you at the gym. You were on the rings! "That is your Dad," she said. Mom took me to see you because I kept asking her about you. When you and others were done performing, we finally met. You promised you would meet me back at the place where you practiced on the rings. You were going to show me how to perform on the rings! I was so happy and excited! God Bless you Dad. Do you know how good I felt just to be around you?

Over time you showed me how to exercise so I would be strong enough to perform on the rings. Handstands against the wall at first until I could learn to walk on my hands. All kinds of exercises to make me strong enough for training me on the rings. You showed me Dad, you showed me how to do the exercises. This would be insignificant to most people. It is very significant to me. My one and only Dad showed me instead of telling me how to do things. Our Father in heaven shows me how to do things instead of telling me how to do things.

This is how I know the difference between my Dad and the fake Dad Drift.

I know the difference between Our Father and the fake our fathers too.

My real Dad was good at swimming. Guess what Dad, me too. I remembered meeting with you at an indoor swimming pool near the same gym where you performed on the rings. I know how much strength it takes to perform a full routine on the rings. I know how good it is for us to go swimming once in a while. I want to thank you for throwing Drift and Eva in the Lake when you visited me. They told me who you were Dad. They told me because you pissed them off.

GOD BLESS YOU DAD

You are an inspiration to me.

Our story will be easy to understand for others now that I wrote it down.

They will reveal our story to others and add their stories to our story. We are all family.

I hope it will resonate with others as it did for you and me.

Mom helped me write to you, so you knew what I was doing. We folded up the letter I wrote to you and we put it in an addressed envelope. I licked the stamp and placed it in the appropriate corner. Then we walked to the corner with the post box. Mom picked me up and I put the letter in the box for you Dad. I Love You Dad!

I remember you entertaining me before I went to bed with your hands. You would turn my lampshade so the wall became bright. You used your hands to make different shapes between the light and the wall.

You called it a 'Light Show' or you would ask me, 'Are you ready for the best Puppet Show On Earth?' It is a great memory for me. I remember most of the shows you performed for me on the wall. You did it so I would be happy I was with you and then I could settle down before I went to sleep. Only you did this for me. Thank you for trying so hard and for so long.

My Dad called me 'the moth' because I needed a night light. He also called me this because if there were bright lights, I was attracted to them, even if the lights hurt my eyes. I am attracted to the light and the light is attracted to me. I was never afraid when I was young and living with my grandparents until they got rid of me. By getting rid of me, they invited a lot of bad people and bad memories into my life. I was still drawn to the light and the light to me.

Our Father made me strong enough to get through it all. I am here, you can touch me to see if I am real! I am intact, with memories of my family that I received from Our Father in Heaven.

STROLLING DOWN MEMORY LANE

I remember going to the beach with a picnic basket.

The picnic basket had a spot for red and white wine so mom could decide.

Dad and I went looking for canvas and we found a whole bunch of it and we put it in a storage garage. It was fun to be with my Dad and even more fun to help him.

Mom took me to her art classes. My real Mom drove a car! She drove lots of cars!

I loved cars and could tell what car was going by for my Mom and Dad.

Dad had a workout room with every conceivable row your boat machine, weight machine, leg lift, wall mounted weights, workout mats, someone even had a trapeze setup in their backyard?

How many people have a trapeze with a safety net in their backyard?

How many people travel with picnic baskets full of food and drink in their car all the time just in case we have to drive to a house where we get out of the car, go through a house, through the backyard and into the backyard of another house, go in the house, go in the garage and into another car with everyone including the picnic basket. We wait a little while and take off again. How many people have to go through this when someone is following them and will not leave us alone. This happened to us a few times when I was young.

We had houses all over.

Mom packed up some sandwiches and sometimes I helped. I liked to help you Mom. I liked it when you asked me to help, not when you told me to do something. It still doesn't work for me to be told what to do. I have to let things come to me, or I do not go along with the plan.

Dad always came by when he could. Your visits are paramount to me, especially when you brought sister along. I used to do the same thing with Arizona. Meet him at a beach, meet him at a park, meet him at his Mom's to pick him up and to drop him off. Oh the drama with Arizona's Mom.

Sound familiar at all?

I remember ignoring you both because I felt you let me down. I didn't talk to anyone. It wasn't your fault, neither one of you. I love it that you are my Mom and Dad! I love it that I remembered you and my sister and the twins, I never knew until I started looking about another brother.

Hello to all my sisters and brothers, God Bless You All.

I remember the telegrams, don't know what they said, but I knew you were near.

Anything you sent me with very few exceptions, was given to Drift and Eva's relatives. The car, gifts, cards, telegrams, candy, anything. Or it was sold, like the car. No one forgets a brand new Z28, not even me. When I drove the car once, I was about 17 years old. It felt great!

The guitar you gave me was replaced with a Sears guitar that someone wrecked the strings on. I played yours and was never hurt like that, but when Drift and Eva switched guitars, my fingers bled. I stopped playing the guitar for years because of them, not you Dad. One of them ripped the strings so that they cut my fingers. Nice people huh?

The musical instruments you sent went to Drifts' brothers who sucked at playing them.

I showed them how easy it was to play them. They sold all of them. I played on the guitar for a few minutes until they kicked me out of the basement where they were making horrible noises.

Pretty damned arrogant considering they were playing gifts given to me.

I saw you go by in your trick cars Dad. I knew it was you, I am completely sure now.

I remember the house with the musical instruments. I remember your friends who played.

The same house had a closet with trophies in it. When you opened the closet door, so many trophies were stuffed into the closet that they poured out all over you. I liked all the instruments, the trombone, the trumpet, the bass, the guitar, the piano, all of them, but the drums are my favorite instrument and the one I play most naturally!

I remember the phase shifter hooked up through the drums. It sounded real cool!

I know you and Mom didn't like the way things happened to me.

I remember bringing Mom breakfast in bed.

I remember making mimosas with and without.

Oh how I loved the ocean. It killed me to take me away from the ocean.

Never mention why I forgot you, or blocked you out or whatever.

Maybe we can talk about that sometime? When we are in a different state of mind?

Do you know how many times Our Father in Heaven saved me? It is how I remembered you. It took a lot of times.

I am made of the very best stuff on earth.

I am here on earth to make things right again with my family.

Only my real Father would give me a money tree as a birthday gift, so I could give my son one too. Arizona was old enough to know money does not grow on trees, but he liked it!

I'm so sorry you got hurt when we went off the parking ramp, please forgive me Dad?

I'm so sorry you passed already. Now I know you would have believed me. You believe in me.

I prayed for sister to get better before she even got real ill. I see things in the future but I have no way of letting any of you know what is going to happen, so I pray to keep you safe and of course Our Father answers every time.

I was the first one to ride shotgun in your cars Dad and I unwillingly shared my seat with my sister. Thank you for reminding us that you loved us both!

I remember everyone showing me the key in a rock. Everyone told me the same thing, "If you ever want to get in, you are always welcome, we only show family where the key is hiding".

One by one my family would show me where they hid the house key. First my Mom, then my Dad, then my little sister. At other homes it was Nana, Grandma and Grandpa. Same at Dad's folks. It was so fun to follow you and that you whispered what you told me. Don't tell anyone.

Mom, I am sorry I shared the joke with you that I read on a Dixie cup in the downstairs bathroom at the beach home.

Thank You Dad for the Tiger's Eye

Thank you Dad, for trying to give me a mini bike in Menomonie Wisconsin. I went back to that park at Lake Menomin, in Menomonie Wisconsin. The Drive-In theater is gone, but the park is still there. Even the road we met on is a tar road now.

It sure was nice of you to think of me. Thank You Dad! I really wanted one too.

There is one gift you gave to me that no one can take away from me. It is your visits! You already visited me. You were seen by plenty of my classmates. They told me when you came and they saw you talking and playing catch or tennis with me. They wished they had a Dad like you. They wanted to meet you! Cool huh?

Oh the mysterious ways of Our Father, how I love it when it is understandable to me.

There is one gift Our Father in Heaven gave me that no one can take away from me.

The Bright White Light and that it showed me my life.

So that I could remember your visits! Thank You to all my Fathers.

Thank You to all my Mothers. Thank you.

I am making a good show.

CHAPTER SIX

Brothers and Sister

To my Sister. I know where you can see lady slippers in Wisconsin. It is where Dad brought you to play with me when we were little. Do you remember playing on the teeter totter in Las Vegas or Lake Havasu before I left for Wisconsin?

I cannot thank you enough for visiting me in a taxi cab. I remembered! No one can take away the gifts you gave to me when you visited me. Another visitor, my sister, I love you for this.

I remember trying to play yard games with your friends. Egg in a spoon, roll an egg, freeze tag.

I remember you showing me your doll house and telling me all the furniture you were going to put in it. I told you I could make you some furniture.

I remember watching TV with you.

I'm sorry I broke your glass horse, or was it a unicorn, whichever, sorry.

Do you remember the picture on the wall of the stairway landing? I'm back in the picture!

I pedaled the pedal car for you, I tried to show you but your legs weren't long enough.

It was your cigarette in the closet, not mine. I am the one who got it for you. Who took the fall for you. Mom was so easy to fool. Hope you didn't get like that.

I sang a lullaby to you when you were first home for our family Christmas. It helped you sleep. I didn't know it at the time, but our whole family was watching. God Bless Our Whole Family.

I used to push you on the swing until Mom interrupted. I know you liked it when I pushed you on the swing because I loved to be pushed on a swing.

Tea parties at Grandma's were a lot of fun with you around. Not as much fun with your friends.

Your taxi ride offer stands in my mind as the best show of loyalty.

Your taxi ride to visit me was paramount! Everyone who visits me is special to me.

I will pick lady slippers with you any time they are in season, around August. You know where.

You used to write to me. Pen pals I believe the term was called.

I gave you some honey suckle flowers and showed you how to get the nectar.

I wrote a whole play called Musical Chairs for you. At the end it has a lady slipper on a chair for you to pick! I thought you would like to see a lady slipper again and maybe your older brother.

Hey! Pick one or both? Is it legal to pick a brother? Is there a legal way to pick a brother?

I have finished ten paintings to mark each chapter of my life.

To my brothers, I only met the twins. I changed your diapers with help from our sister. Mom was busy on the phone or getting ready to be somewhere. It was when I was on a visit. You guys were full of energy but played nice in your play pen most of the time. You also had a way of moving the entire playpen across the floor. You worked in tandem from the very start. It was great to watch! To the brothers and sisters I have not met yet. I am named after Grandpa Gorilla. You could call me a grease monkey, because for a long time I greased the squeaky wheels. I'm tired of that, so I learned how to read and write. I'm a cross between, curious George, Harold and all the crayons and Casper the friendly ghost. Boo!

Grandma Jane liked to look in the mirror and think things over. She did show sister and I the attic with her chest full of memories! Hey you guys, did our sister ever tell you about the house with the hidden pull down stairway? The house had a name. Did you get to go in the attic?

To you all. Dad used to show me the 8 sign, but on its side. I called it 'the racetrack' and he would laugh. "no", he said, "not a racetrack, it means something else and he told me what it means. It is a symbol for eternity. It fit right in with my favorite number 00. He showed me so long ago with a stick in the sand. You see, my grandpa was 98, my uncle would be 99, which

would make me 100, but there is not enough room for '100' on a jersey, so I loved the number 00. I remembered my first favorite number was 00. It is a racetrack too, sort of.

My sister was the first person I knew since she was born and now we have lost track of each other. It will be in God's time that we find each other again.

God Bless All of You, To all of my brothers and sisters, Thank You!

Your Brother,
Drift Lucky Walker or Gorilla "The Grease Monkey" McGillicudy Kidd?
I think I will go with Lucky!
I hope you are all making a good show.

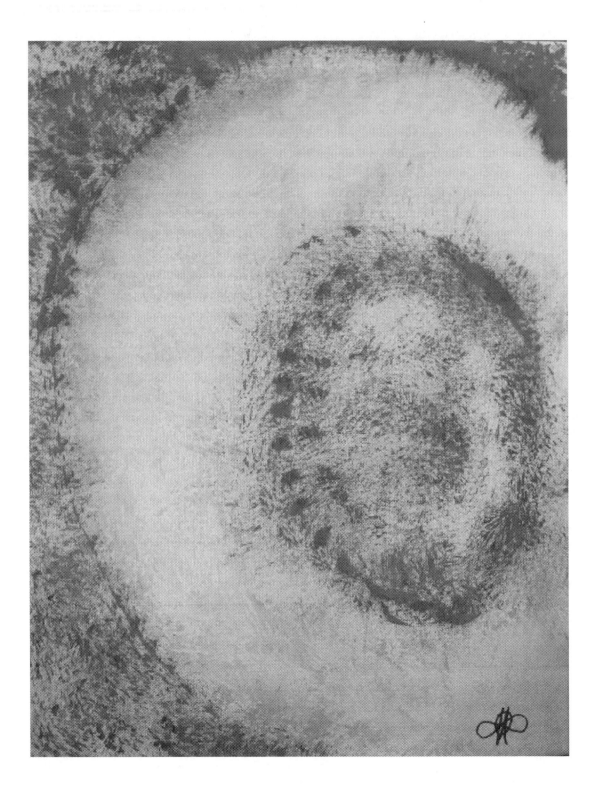

CHAPTER SEVEN

Grandparents, Uncles and Aunts

Faith lets me know that people need to be reminded. Faith and I just met, but we know each other very well. We both have a like life. Her Mom raised her and it was not all perfect, but her Mom raised her. Her family loves her and Faith noticed the same things I have noticed in my life.

Faith asked me if I have reminded the reader how I received my memories. Refer to the Bright White Light at the beginning of this book. It should be clear who reminded me and that I am Thankful.

Even I took a long time to remember all of this. Since my memories go back to very early childhood, many will have difficulty believing me. It's okay, it took me a long time to believe it all myself. If Our Father had not intervened, I would have no memories of this, but I do.

Do you remember your childhood?

This Chapter is for all of my ancestors, all of my Fathers, Mothers and everyone who came here before me. Hey, Uncles and Aunts too! I received all of my memories.

I remembered playing Musical Chairs in a school uniform. All the other kids I was playing with had school uniforms too! That is when I started to remember people from my early childhood.

My great Grandmother was the first person I remembered. She did everything for me! In the early morning hours my 'Nana' had a whistling teapot that we all heard. It was our whole families alarm clock. I heard it without fail since my bedroom was at the top of the stairs next to the bathroom. I was too little to use the bathroom. I used to crawl in the bathroom and look around for a little while. What did they do in here?

There was a knock at the door. It was my Mom's sister and she needed the bathroom. I crawled out of the bathroom and down the stairs. My uncle flew by me and down the stairs. He ate pretty fast and out the door he went ahead of everyone! I slowly crawled down the stairs and made way to my high chair. Nana hoisted me up and set me into my high chair. She snapped the tray on the rails and here came my breakfast!

My Great Grandma is 'Nana', I will call her that to save some key strokes.

Within a few minutes, everyone except my uncle was at the table eating. My uncle was out the door for something at school. We ate together for breakfast and dinner every day.

After breakfast everyone was somewhere else, except Nana and me. We stayed home every day.

Nana was cleaning up breakfast and I crawled to the window with a padded seat built into it. I was watching for the lawn mower men. I watched and waited for them every day, but they only showed up when the plants needed attention. It was always fun when the mailman showed up and dropped our mail in our slot. I would crawl over and pick it up and give it to my Nana.

When Nana was done with clean up, she took me to the playroom.

The playroom was almost all white. All the toys were behind white sliding doors. There were two rocking horses in the opposite corner of the door to the room. Nana would walk in the playroom, set me on the carpeted floor, slide open the white door and pull the barn set off the shelf and put it on the floor for me to play with every morning. When I was older, she would let me play with dominoes. I loved my play time. Nana would tell me to 'play like a good boy' and 'I have to go back upstairs and take care of business'. I played alone with no other kids. I would sit in the window and stare outside looking for other kids, the lawn mower men, the milkman, anyone!

When Nana was busy, I was alone.

We would eat lunch every day. After lunch I was taken upstairs to take a nap. Nana would read to me sometimes. She read Bible Stories. Noah had a big boat and a lot of pets. Moses kept trying to get home, but was lost most of the time until Our Father helped him get home. Moses was so impressed with the help that he wrote some of the stories down so all of us could read them. Jesus was trying to get a message through to us, but they stopped him before he could write it all down. At a dinner, Jesus asked his trusted and closest friends to write it down for him. They did write it down and we were reading some of it. Nana is the best!

Thank you for reading me stories about our relatives who were here before us Nana, God Bless You.

I wanted to learn how to read.

I wanted to learn how to write.

I wanted to play with kids my age.

I wanted to play with anyone. I tried to play with the piano tuner man, but he had work to get done. He showed me his neat shiny forks. He touched the forks and listened to the sound when he touched the keys. I tried with the lawn mower men, but Nana said the machines and tools were too dangerous. One day I got past her and outside. Wow! What a place! Fresh air, birds, bees, trees swaying all kinds of noises! The lawn mower men coaxed me back to the door. 'Nada bambino' Not bad, just in the wrong place. So I stayed inside for the lawn mower men from then on. Nana had to explain to me why it was dangerous again. I stayed inside.

Sometimes they would put me in the attic when certain people would visit. I would watch out the window and see people coming into the house. I don't know who they were. The good part of being in the attic was that I could see all around the house without anyone stopping me.

It is how I knew there were other children.

It is how I knew we lived in a neighborhood with other houses.

It is how I learned about my family.

My Grandma Jane had a hope chest she stored upstairs in the attic. Grandma's hope chest had all of her memories inside. When I was older, Grandma showed my sister and I what was inside. That is private and I hope to talk about it when we meet up. It is nothing to be ashamed of, I think I can share this one item. The item was Grandma's wedding dress. I can share that since my Mom told the world about Grandma's Holy wedding dress.

My Mother has a hope chest. Mother's sister has a hope chest. My sister has a hope chest.

Nana had a trunk. It used to be her hope chest. She had to use it to bring everything precious with her to this new place. All of my Mother's side women have these hope chests. It is where they store all of their precious memories.

Our attic was hard to get to. You had to find the hidden stairs in the ceiling.

Nana did not go up there because she was not comfortable climbing a stair ladder anymore. I loved it and wished I could live up there and climb up and down the stairway all day!

These are my memories of what happened around me before I was three years old. They are centered around my Great Grandmother, Nana.

Riding the vacuum cleaner and humming along with the noise it made as Nana cleaned up the house. She would laugh and told me to, 'Get off my horsy so she could get her housework done'. She would wiggle and pull the vacuum hose around and I would laugh trying to hold on.

Nana taught me how to set the table and after we ate, how to clean up dishes.

Nana taught me how to dust all the furniture.

Nana taught me how to read and write.

Nana taught me how to put on my clothes and how to fold them and put them away.

My first memory was playing Musical Chairs, my second memory was my school uniform, my third memory was that someone laid out my school uniform for me. It was Nana!

Nana told my Grandpa how bad his idea was to get rid of me. Nana said 'there were other ways' the night before he took me away. Grandpa took me to an orphanage. This is where the bad people entered my life.

Up to that point, I knew my Grandpa had mixed feelings about me, but I never thought he would do that to me.

It does not matter what your status is in society. One thing no one should ever be ashamed of is their family. Status and society are not living things in my world.

Faith shared it with me this morning and it was so obvious to me why there is such a force behind me to write this all down.

Faith said, "You are spanking the hand of society". I have another way to put it. Because of how society treated me, I would like to punch society right in the face! It is what society gave me with no way out! I tried to get away from the two pigs that beat the shit out of me and society, the police and our justice system put me right back with them. Can you blame me for being angry. For saying children have no rights? Please remember who gave me my memories back. I am bound by my promise to Our Father to share these stories about my family. They are precious to me. I did not write any of this to offend them, I am writing this down so they know I remembered them. I will not hurt anyone who does not hurt me or my family.

Had I felt like part of my family I would not be writing down my memories for them to read. We would be talking about current, past and future stories together like most families. But we do not do that. I am doing this to share the most important part of my story. The most important part of my story is who gave me my memories back and that I am thankful for it.

Thank You to the Bright White Light and to Our Father in Heaven. I am so grateful.

I hope you like that I finally remembered and believed this all myself. I believe it all because I only believe in you. Thank you for helping me write it down. It was too hard to do myself.

It is the only way I know how to do things, you know, to write it all down. I paint and have a particular painting done already of the house I visited in Wisconsin. It is the two pillars at the gate of the driveway. The house is a private residence that used to be a meeting place for my Dad, my sister and I in 1968-1969. I hope you recognize the pillars.

My Grandfathers were entrenched in society. I remember them saying, "This will destroy everything we have, everything we know, everything we worked so hard for, he has to go". This is how things were, it was how our culture treats children who were born to soon. They keep it simple, you get rid of them! I saw children no one wanted at the orphanage, I saw children that were given away by their families. No one visited them. I was Lucky to get out. Believe me.

This is how I see it all. There is the old way, the way of my Grandparents and there is the new way of my Father. The meeting places like the one I visited in Wisconsin, represent the new way of my Father because it is where we met. Our Father brought my sister, his brother, both of my Grandma's visited me, but never my Mom or her Father. Once I was gone, they didn't look back. Dad told me they have the ways they believe and they are entitled to believe that way.

Our Father in heaven rules over them and keeps them safe just like he does you and me. My story would have had no drama, no emotion to be of any interest without my Grandfathers' catering to the 'all-important society'.

I told them both that I could beat them with one arm tied behind my back, with a broken leg, with my body beaten and my will tired from the years of battling the old ways. I told my Mom's Dad this when I was three and my Dad's Dad at four years old.

They laughed at me and Grandpa Gorilla took me away. They gave me to people who tortured me in order to scare me into doing what they wanted me to do. One bad decision led to another, which led to another bad decision, which led to another, and another and another. This went on until I was about to turn forty years old in 2001. I was separated from my family before I turned four years old.

I remembered all of this when I was thirty nine years old with the help of Our Father in Heaven.

I am writing this down at fifty three years old. Does anyone think I am rushing into this?

I will see my whole family at home in heaven. It would be nice to see them here before we meet again back home, but my attempts seem to reach no one. I wanted to keep this secret and still let them know I was okay. Somehow I thought it would work that way, but my family has been passing away one by one, I do not want to wait any longer.

HERE IS A PIE IN ALL OF YOUR FACES

I remember opening up the darkroom door when I was visiting my Dad's Dad, Maurice. If you are under thirty years old, ask anyone older what film used to be. Believe it or not, you had to develop it in a special, 'darkroom'.

I remember sitting in the director's chair that belonged to Maurice. I was warned by my family.

I remember what Maurice said to me when I was in his chair and what I said back to him.

I remember him showing me how to thread a projector and splice film.

I remember him showing me how to do sound effects.

I remember him typing in his office just like my other Grandpa.

I remember both Grandpa's being gone quite often.

I remember the good things you did mostly and know I will see you again.

My uncle reminds me of Flash Gordon. Now you see him, now you don't. Somehow I know my uncle will remember that he put together or fastened wood blocks to a pedal car that would be another verification for me. A good one too. To my mother's brother, God Bless You.

Nana is the one who told my sister and I who made the pedal car, or who fixed the car so we could use it. Thank you Uncle. Want to play a game of full contact tetherball?

My Aunt, my mom's sister is pretty just like my Mom. When she took me places, men would whistle at her too. I told them in my own way to knock it off. Do you remember? Who took me to movies? My Aunt took me to movies. I would write to you, but what do I say? I always thought you were on a photo shoot taking the pictures, not the picture they were taking. I know we were able to get Chevy's because of you. I wish we could meet again. Let me know through the grapevine.

Someone sent me a brand new 1978 Camaro Z28. I drove it to Next to This Town Wisconsin and back to This Town. Twenty miles and Drift and Eva sold it! I don't know who sent it, I was grateful then even though I believed the BS Drift and Eva told me. I know better now. I never received anything from any of you when I was being raised by them. They took everything away. I may have held it for a few minutes or less and then Drift and Eva packed it up and shipped it to their relatives or sold it.

Every once in a while I received and enjoyed your gifts, I enjoyed them for the time I was able to enjoy them. Knowing that you all sent cards, telegrams, gifts, a car, everything you sent me is now known to me. I remember people who give me gifts forever. God Bless You.

Writing this is the best way I know how to reach anyone at this point in my life. It is the only gift I can share until we meet again. I hope you thoroughly enjoy reading it.

I remember when my Auntie and my Mom saw the Admiral's son coming down the walk. You were both watching him get closer to the door. You two were pretty excited to meet him. He gave me a pipe whistle. It sort of sounded like Popeye's whistle.

You see, while everyone was watching someone else, I was watching all of you. It was all I had to do. I wanted to be a reporter since I was very young. Here I am reporting. All that wasted time getting a ladder, a periscope, opera glasses, a pen, some paper, where is a camera? If I would have had a camera back then, I would have and gotten into trouble for it too.

Does anyone remember going to the music store and buying 45's?

Does anyone remember playing 45's on their portable record players?

You are my Aunt and you rode one of the rocking horses that I always wanted to ride. I can see you and Mom riding side by side when you were little in my mind, what fun.

Someone promised me a pony. I weigh more than a pony now, so I guess that let's someone off the hook? Not off the hook completely though. A big pony would be funny, maybe I could ride an ass down main street? Can I even say 'Hee Haw!'

If you play tug-of-war, you want me on your team. Even if it is me on one side and all of you on the other side, I know who will win. Does anyone remember playing tug-of-war? I do.

The Beach

The Clear Water

The Boat Rides

The Mountain Cabin

I live in an RV. I travel wherever I need to now, to live and enjoy my life. I am where I am today because of Our Father in Heaven, Our Fathers, Our Mothers and I am thankful, no matter how angry I have been about all this, I am grateful and thankful now.

I have a son named Arizona as you know by the third chapter of this book. He is just like my Dad. He looks like him, talks like him, walks like him and sings like him. Of course he is young and I am letting him do whatever he wants to do. I am trying to show him what to do without telling him what to do. I hope he sees the show I am making, so he can make a good show.

To Grandpa and 'Don't Call Me Pops', Grandpa:

You did a great job, both of you. Someone had to be r-e-s-p-o-n-s-i-b-l-e, right?

There are a lot of kids just like me who had a bad decision made for them and they have no way out in their minds because of how one bad decision leads to another. We feel buried. But some of us can get out of it, we know who helped us too, and we are very thankful to Our Father.

You see, if one bad thing can lead to another, then good things can lead to other good things, which can lead to more good things, which leads us to more good things and so on!

I try to see the good with who I am and what I was presented with.

Do you think Noah would have turned away a bastard child of his in order to further his family and in turn, our family? What does society have to say about a rising flood? Nothing, they are swimming for their lives! If they can swim. All the money and status in the world cannot save you when the time comes. This is specifically for society and my mom's side of my family.

Even at the expense of being laughed at, Noah would have been grateful to have family aboard his ship. Noah would have been grateful to take any plants, animals, food, water, music to pass the time and maybe a story teller for telling stories of our ancestors? He would have been happy to include all these things because he was fulfilling his mission and his promise to Our Father.

I am fulfilling my promise and I think this is a good start to sharing my stories. It is really up to him and how he sees things through me and you. I have way more stories about my family. I could probably write a book for each chapter of this book!

Our Father in Heaven is family too you know. We are all connected by our Mother Earth too! Where would we be without the Bright White Light so that we can see?

I am not sorry to discuss any Bible Stories. Anyone wishing to argue whether they are important or not should understand how important they are to me. My family, my Nana, my Dad, my Mom, my Mom's folks and if I missed you, Thank You to all who read to me, because only my real family read Bible Stories to me when I was very young from the same books read to them.

There are many classmates that I met over the years because of how often we had to move. If you have stories to share, let me know. I will add your memories to the next book.

The gateway to my family has been reopened since 2001 thanks to Our Father in Heaven. Our Father had to keep trying to get through to me and he never gave up. You see, I never asked for any of my memories to come back to me. I did see them many times before they stuck in my head. It is stuck good enough now and I am strong enough to go forward.

I am sticking to my Promise made to Our Father. I hope you see the good like I do.

Thank You,
Lucky McGillicudy Kidd!
Lucky will suffice
Lucky I'm making a good show like my Dad's side of the family.

CHAPTER EIGHT

For My Classmates and Friends, "Life is a Trip"

I wore a raincoat and boots to school quite often. Someone drove me to school every day. I never rode a bus to school until after we moved to Wisconsin. I had a lunchbox that was filled with plenty of everything I liked every day. I wore the same shirt as the other boys. The same tie, slacks and only dark socks, preferably blue socks. I would often put on a black sock on my left foot and a blue sock on my right foot. I wanted to be different, I didn't want to look like everybody else. My first school had Nuns, but not any flying Nun hats. They sure liked to tell me what do all the time. I brought them gifts and they still had a problem being nice to me. Musical Chairs is named after my years at this school. It is where I played 'Musical Chairs'. It is my first memory. I cannot find the school, but I looked all over for it.

Most of us know the game of musical chairs, Musical Chairs is a game of elimination and only one person wins. I was so anxious to play with other kids because I was not allowed to play with anyone until I went to school. I was told the story of how school was so fun. Of how all the kids my age were learning and playing with kids our own age. My Great Grandmother told me 'kinder' meant children and that 'garten' meant garden in German. This school must not have known what my Great Grandmother knew and shared with me. They wanted us to do boring worksheets and go to the blackboard and draw a letter or a number. Come on, it was boring. Kindergarten was hardly a 'Children's Garden'.

We played Duck, Duck Gray Duck; We played London Bridge Is Falling Down; We played lots of games at school. We only played one game a day for about five minutes after the Nun was done explaining, "How to Play"

Whichever Nun was in charge of the game always went over the rules in depth.

"What we should be thinking when we play".

"How we should feel when we are playing the game".

"What the total strategy is to win the game and how we should feel if we won or lost".

"How to run safely", Joanie could you show us how nice and safely you run? "Thank You".

"What we should say and what we should do at the same time to play the game correctly".

They didn't want us to play and have fun. They just wanted us to feel like we played and had fun. We hardly ever played. It was learn our abc's and 123's, I already knew this stuff. Our teacher always promised to let us play and have fun. Promises are different then someone coming through for you. I learned more by playing than I ever learned in a classroom.

At home it was the same thing. Rules, Work, What I had to do for them. All the while I knew they were planning to get rid of me. I heard them and understood what they were saying about me. The first few times I heard it, I tied a noose around my neck and kicked a chair out from under my feet. The Bright White Light found me and put me into my bed.

I heard my own Grandparents discussing what they had to do, they had to get rid of me.

What happened next was just my frustration over what was and had been happening to me.

We finally had a chance to play a whole game and it didn't take too long to explain. It went fast and it had music included, in fact as an important role for the game to be fun and exciting. I won the second round. The teacher showed me how to put the needle on the record and back up again without scratching or damaging the record. Guess how long that took me to realize she was going to take way too long again. She just had to show me over and over until I started to drift. I sat and watched as though it was information that would lead me to a successful moon shot of which I was the only astronaut on board…

Her explaining things allowed me to be creative, I took the best out of the situation. I drifted into a world of make believe. It is how I coped with their 'destructions', you heard me right, not 'Instructions', DESTRUCTIONS. It pays to be able to travel somewhere else when you need to.

Finally after what seemed to be about ten minutes, the Nun let me start the next round of 'Musical Chairs'.

The music stopped, they all sat down except one. Could someone please pull away a chair?

Next round, the music stops, they all sit down except one. Wow was I having fun!

That game had a winner and I was all ready to win the next round so I could play the music.

After a few rounds of the music stopping, it was down to a few people, the girl next to me and myself.

The Music Stopped. We tried to find and get into a chair before we were the one to be eliminated.

I pushed my way into a chair when the music stopped. A girl was trying for the same chair. I was trying to be gentle, but I was trying to 'win' and the girl did not hit the seat of the chair as solid as I did. She was bumping into the side of me after my ass hit the chair! I was punished? Now I was pissed off. My punishment was no lunch. This made me more pissed off. I spent my lunch writing something like, "I will not hurt others when we are playing games."

My attitude then is the same as it is now. I sat in the chair first because I was faster, the girl tried harder than I did, but she bounced off of me and landed on the floor. She is the one who played rough, not me. I had to brace myself on the chair to keep it!

I was punished for being aggressive while playing 'Musical Chairs'. The girl was not hurt, she was just on the floor wishing she was on the chair. She was not mad at me, she was mad that she lost! The teacher was mad at me though! She made a big deal out of nothing as usual to me. I wrote what she wanted me too on the blackboard until she was out of sight.

I saw an open window and pushed a chair over to it. I pushed the window open a little more and crawled out. I was hungry and nothing fun happened in the classroom anyway. The teacher always punished me for every little thing. She did not understand that I never got to play with other kids. The details are unclear, but I know it was not long after that incident that a decision was made that would change my life.

When I first met my new adoptive parents, they had to re-enroll me at my old school. They took me to the school and when they saw that it cost money to re-enroll me, they created a big scene. They dragged me out of there as if I had done something wrong. Oh how I hated my life back then.

They took me to another kindergarten school and enrolled me. It was the best school because it was free.

This may seem like an unimportant thing to remember, but it is significant. My real folks paid for my schooling the first year I went to school. My real folks had no problems with the cost.

Drift and Eva were only interested in getting the money from my parents and putting it in their pockets. Drift and Eva were hardly going to take the money you gave them and do anything positive for me.

It was even worse the second time around for kindergarten. Now I was with the wrong parents. They packed me a brown bag lunch with a peanut butter sandwich and on rare occasion, maybe a banana or apple. I hate peanut butter sandwiches and apples! These two people were into giving me the opposite of what I wanted at all costs! I was their 'meal ticket' and my Dad was the Goose who laid the golden egg!

I have been in touch with classmates that saw me with my father Nevada Kidd. Many have come forward. Some do not mind if I use their names. Chuck and many of my classmates at my Elementary School, Junior High School and High School. They saw me with my Grandparents, Maurice and Charlotte Kidd and my Dad! Before my Classmates saw my real family, they treated me as just another boy in class. After they saw my real family with me, they treated me differently. Our house phone rang off the hook. Kids that didn't care about me before were now calling to invite me to their birthday party, sleepover, out to eat to meet their parents. Thank you for taking an interest. Thank you to all for contributing and helping me.

God Bless You.

Ms./Mrs. Goode for Kindergarten and Ms./Mrs. Cooper for First Grade.

I wonder if any classmates that went to my kindergarten and first grade with me remember me as the kid who saw my Dad and went to pull the fire alarm. I was in a walking sleep. For some reason whenever I saw him after I was adopted, I would over react. The reason was all the programming I received from Drift and Eva. This time was no different. My Dad pulled up and parked near the crosswalk by our kindergarten classroom. He was trying to wake me up again. He told me he loved me and he wished I would come home with him.

I was afraid of him. I went and pulled the fire alarm and the firemen and fire trucks came to the rescue! Unfortunately another failed attempt at trying to wake me up. I was afraid of him because Drift and Eva showed me pictures of him and called him bad names. I was delirious when they did this to me. I know that now.

Does anyone remember that I put tacks on Mrs. Coopers Chair? I put a few tacks on her chair and she sat on them. She didn't wince or anything. After a minute or so, the kids in our class started giggling at first. The giggling turned into outright laughter when Mrs. Cooper figured it out. She wiggled around and up and out of her chair!

Mrs. Cooper humiliated me and made an example of me the day before. Since no one stood up for me, I had to stand up for me. She put me in the middle of the classroom with a Dunce Hat on a higher chair than my Classmates. She deserved the tacks.

Anyone want to say hello? We went to school together in 1966-1967 and 1967-1968 years. We would have graduated in 1979 or 1980? I was held back at Drift and Eva's demands, under duress. They threatened me by telling me what would happen if I didn't stay in 5th grade. They followed through on their threats with me and they enjoyed doing bad things to me.

In June of 1968, right before school was over for the year, we packed up the trailer for Wisconsin. My sister showed up at our house in Las Vegas. A taxi cab pulled up and there she was opening the door to get out! She called out to me and I ran up to her. She wanted me to take her to a private place so we went to the backyard. Our backyard consisted of garages. We agreed to go to the neighboring set of garages when we remembered my adoptive mother Eva might be spying on us. My blood Sister wanted me to remember her. I do now and since 2002. We talked about how I would be sure it was her and that she was sure it was me when we met somewhere down the line.

My real sister will remember what we did, said and promised to each other forever that day.

The next school I attended was in Wisconsin, Whatever… It is closed and they gave me no records of attendance, in fact, no records at all just proof I went there. The year was 1968-69. Ms. French was my second grade teacher. I know some of you saw me visiting my Dad in this gated community. Thank you to Dallas from Texas for contributing. God Bless You. The first classmate to tell me who I was with when he saw me visit my Dad. It was the house with the two pillars. The house and the pillars are still there.

Next stop was This Town Elementary in Wisconsin. Ms./Mrs. Hanson for third grade. The year was 1969-70.

My Dad brought me a laughing bag. His brother came along to. Every time Eva or Drift said something, you squeezed it and it laughed! Oh I love that memory too.

One time they drove a dune buggy, One time you drove a Jaguar, One time you drove a Road Runner. One time you threw my adoptive parents in the water off the dock at the Lake! May God Bless You Forever Dad! Thank you for doing that to them, they deserved that and a whole lot more.

I started fourth grade at This Town Elementary and we moved again. Now we went to school at Another Town Elementary in St. Something in Wisconsin. Ms./Mrs. Tuskegee was my fourth grade teacher. I was a flash card master back then in 1970-71. My Classmates would remember the effort I made to say the answers the second the flash card was turned with a multiplication problem to solve. They may remember me by my drumming on Bongos with Alphonse Milleski for a Talent Contest. Al's brothers knew who I was as did his Mom. Then came fifth grade in 1971-72 and Ms./Mrs. Hahnsen. My adoptive parents moved and supposedly Eva was pregnant. We moved again but just across the greenway between apartment buildings to the other apartment building.

I know you watched me play football. The only thing coaches want on their team is kids Dad's that they want to work with, not how good of a player they are, that is unimportant. They should have paid more attention to how much I loved football.

I played organized baseball in the spring for the first time and loved it like crazy! One day when I was playing alone in St. Something Park, my Dad showed up again! He had a friend with this time. We walked and talked. He asked if I knew how to 'play ball'? "I sure did!" I let him know he could wait there and I would go get some gloves, a ball, a bat, whatever I could find and then I ran back! We played catch and he pitched me some balls. Oh how he was trying to get me to remember him. I love you Dad for meeting me out-of-the-blue. It is what is driving me to complete my mission and write this all down.

Thank You Dad

Thank You to my real Dad on earth and in heaven and all the Dad's before us!

Thank You to Our Father, Dad to all for helping me so much.

Our phone rang off the hook again! You don't know how much I wanted to go to your birthday parties, sleepover, tennis matches, whatever you wanted to do, we would have had fun. Drift and Eva would not take me to your events and as for the ones I went to? I went to a few but ran out of money to buy more gifts. So I unwillingly had to decline your wonderful invitations.

Thank you to all of you for being so nice to me back then. I think it was great what you did, because I remembered all of you, it helped me remember my family.

May God Bless All Of You for your efforts.

In 1972-73 my teacher was Ms. Kidd for fifth grade the second time around at my adopted parents demand. Can you believe that? She had the same last name as my Dad and I never put it together before I wrote this down. Drift and Eva threatened me with what would happen to me if I did not stay in fifth grade. Mr. Green the principal knew something was odd about my request.

I told him I was too small to go to sixth grade. He agreed to let me go through fifth grade again, unhappily and under protest. He asked me over and over again through the year, but I didn't change my mind. Why would I change my mind? I would have to be taught a lesson again by Drift and Eva. I would have to be taught a lesson and be punished for going to the next grade. I earned going to the next grade! I was very good at Reading, Writing and Arithmetic. I was a two year crossing guard which meant I had to get up early. I never missed a day of school. My reward was to be held back so I could do it again?

1973-74 I started Sixth grade Mr. Wilson. I could thread the film projector before I went to kindergarten. How did I know how to do this? Because I saw my Grandfather thread the 'cutter'. The cutter is a film projector with a 'cutter' in the middle to splice two pieces of film. I knew how to do that too. I set up a listening station for almost our whole class to listen to records! It was great. This was the class that forced me into a confrontation. Me facing the class and I would not back down from my argument. Anyone remember me at Yet Another Town Elementary? I stood my ground and we all were able to listen to music.

I know my Dad was around because the neighbor kids I knew were trying to tell me you were looking for me. Here I am Dad!

I finished sixth grade at Even Another Town Elementary in Wisconsin. It was 1974 and the principal, Mr. General Minor Major Richard Head, asked me why I stole the money. Then he asked me if I wanted to tell him anything. My first day of school I was accused of this.

Mrs. Doe. I would not and have never stole money from a teacher's purse and think the way Mr. General Minor Major Richard Head handled it along with everyone else was ridiculous. I do not have anything nice to share with you for your accusation and misjudgment. As for my math teacher who was upset that I took a candy from the dish. Geez, you handed them out to the other kids when they finished one sheet for the whole hour of class! I finished 10-12 sheets in an hour every day and you forgot to give me my one piece of candy many times, you said I could take them as I wanted for all the good work I turned in. So I took it while you were busy with another student. I waited for this teacher for 20 minutes for my reward. I let you know before I took it and after. I let you know that we were square on treats and you accused me of stealing too. I did not steal a piece of candy from any teacher, not even one piece.

1974-75, 75-76, 1976- Crow's Nest Junior High School. I know my eighth grade teachers all remember me. I did something real stupid to get attention. They knew something was wrong and tried to help me. One teacher in particular really singled me out and tried to piss me off. He accomplished his task. To the other teachers who were genuinely concerned, thank you.

Mr. Vice Principal, Thank you for being fair. Either you knew my story or understood it because you took the time to talk to me and listen to what I said.

Thank You to Daniella Kidd who saw me at Lord Fletcher's Apartments in Yet Another Town Wisconsin. Funny, weren't you visiting your Dad too? Do you remember anything? Does anybody remember anything? It is automatically included in my next book if you want to share.

My Dad just showed up on my paper route. His shirt was open because it was hot out. We hopped in to Valley's jet boat docked up near Lord Fletcher's Apartment's. Thank You to the guy at Spur gas station, Young Mr. Mountain with the Olds 442. Thank You and God Bless the Valley's and the Mountain's.

Thank you to Kitty and whoever was with her of Yet Another Town in Wisconsin who all confronted my adoptive mother. Thank You to the High School Talent Contest and my friends who let me drive their car. Nice Monte Carlo! Thank you to your friend the singer/guitar player who came over to play in our garage and who wanted me in your band. You let me drive your Monte Carlo Rich, Thanks Again! God Bless You Kitty, Daniella and Rich.

Thank You to anyone who remembers.

Some of my Classmates in This Town knew my story too. My neighbor JJ figured it out and tried to tell me. I just agreed with you back then to appease you, but now I remember. There is a big difference. Thank You JJ. I also want to Thank You for letting me drive your snowmobile. I was careful with it. Thank You also for introducing me to the people in This Town Close to Our Town west of Ridge Hill. Key to my memories because Dad was around This Town too. My Grandmothers visited too.

Who else knew? Let me know, Thank You!

Your Classmate,
Lucky McGillicudy Kidd
(previously known as Drift Walker)
PS: God Bless You
I like the show you helped me make, Thank You.

CHAPTER NINE

For My Past

Most importantly, Our Father in Heaven helped me with receiving my memories and in writing them down. I am not a writer. I am not an author. I visited my Dad and he visited me. I was helped by the Bright White Light and by Our Father. This was a group effort by my entire family. The fact that my Dad arranged visits back and forth so I could see him and others is very important to me. It is the most important thing besides getting my memories back from Our Father in Heaven.

Most people instantly recognized my Dad or know him as Nevada Kidd.

I just know him as my Dad. My Dad brought his Dad along to visit me, his brother too. First in Lake Havasu, Arizona. Then in Another Town in Arizona and then all the way to Wisconsin. He would pick me up and take me for rides to the beach. To a ranch house in a canyon and not just once.

He visited me at least one hundred times and I visited him too.. Even my Grandma and Grandpa, my Dad's folks, invited me in to their homes. They had homes all over the place too. My other Grandma visited me along with Dad's Mom.

There are good people involved.

Playing My Dad was himself, Nevada Kidd.

My Grandpa played himself, Maurice Kidd.

My Grandma played herself, Charlotte Kidd.

My Dad's brother, played himself as my Uncle.

My Mom is playing herself and her name is Brandy McGillicudy Kidd.

My Mom's Mom, Jane played herself.

My Mom's Dad is Gorilla McGillicudy and he played himself.

My Mom's Brother and sister played themselves as my Uncle and my Aunt.

I almost never remembered any of you without the help from The Bright White Light and Our Father in Heaven who sees through all of us.

Neither one of my Grandmas agreed with Grandpa Gorilla's decision.

Grandpa Gorilla did not want anyone to know I existed and he did the best he could.

All children are innocent, not just the daughters, not just the sons.

I have written to my Mom, Brandy Kidd who told me to call her by her first name.

I have written to my Mom's sister my Aunt McGillicudy and received no reply.

I have written to my Mom's brother, my Uncle McGillicudy and again received no reply.

I do not doubt my heritage on my Father's side of the family. I do not doubt my heritage on my Mom's side. I have faith in the ones who are alive, but after fifty years I am very disappointed that you all gave up trying to wake me up. You are welcome to where I am any time. I am a very good host and Faith is a very good hostess.

I wrote Chapter One for What I remembered from Our Father in Heaven. Because the Bright White Light and Our Father showed me what happened. They showed my life to me from the moment he started sharing all the way back to my birth. I think Our Father in Heaven did this so I could understand and write it all down. This book is only the beginning. I am thankful to Our Father in Heaven.

I wrote Chapter Two for my son Arizona. So he could tell them some of our heritage from before he was born. So he could share the story of our family with the future of our kind. I am writing down what was shown to me from above. I am writing down what I had to go through to be able to write this all down. I am thankful I am made of good stock, because I was put through physical, sexual and mental abuse from the age of three years old on. You see Drift and Eva still want me to believe they are my parents and I better do what they tell me to do. Writing this all down helps me to erase my memories of these two, their families and friends. Thank You.

I wrote Chapter Two for my only son Arizona. Because of Arizona, I was able to stand up and protect him against Drift and Eva. Does anyone know how good it feels to stand up to bullies?

I wrote Chapter Three for Arizona's family and his children to be born. Children are miracles you know. It is not nice to show Our Father in Heaven how unhappy you are with one of his miracles. Miracles happen every day and most of us never notice a thing.

I wrote Chapter Four for the Unbelievers. Unbelievers like to do bad things. They get enjoyment from performing any negative task against people who are positive. They do this because bad decisions were made by or for them and they continued believing there was no hope. You have to see the light before you know it is there. You have to accept the light, but it is everyone's choice to make. You have to be on the right path no matter how difficult and make the best of it! When you continue making bad decisions because you think there is nothing good in this world, you get what you decide.

I wrote Chapter Five for my real Parents, Nevada and Brandy McGillicudy Kidd. My Dad always knew who he was at any given time. My Dad told me he loved my Mom when he made me. He told me when he could not watch over me, that Our Father in Heaven would and Our Father in Heaven did watch over me.

Arizona knows there is someone watching over him all the time. Arizona knows my whole story, but he is young. I am preserving it in writing for him.

My Mom was interested in protecting me when I was young. When her father made it clear she had to give me up, she abided unwillingly. My Mom was a minor and had no rights. I was a child and had no rights either. Children have no rights until eighteen years old now, twenty one years old then. Children and minors are property of our parents. We are property of our government if we have no parents. We are bought and sold, we are given away.

I wrote Chapter Six for my Brothers and Sisters. I only met my twin brothers when they were in diapers. Maybe they can all me 'Rain Man'. Want me to start the rain again?

My sister is the one I believed in to help me out. My brothers were too young to remember me. It would be nice to think they can remember like I do, but I have my doubts. I thought our sister told you about me. If you could help her remember that she came to visit me when she was a little girl. I was only six years old when you came to say visit me to find out we were moving to Wisconsin. That was sweet of you to do for me. My sister and I did a ritual so that we would always be linked. It was at her suggestion. We know what the ritual is.

Hey, speaking of rituals Sister. Could you please reintroduce me to our family so I do not call anyone by the wrong first name? I am pretty sure you know most of them better than I at the moment. It would help me get through some uncomfortable first moments.

Maybe we should all wear name tags? Could we do this before we get to wear toe tags? If we have to wait until toe tags, I would like to design my own toe tag. I am thinking a white gold band with an inscription, 'Here is another ring from another guy who left here only to come back again because it is so difficult to get a simple message through while in paradise.'

I wrote Chapter Seven for my Grandparents, Uncles and Aunts. My Dad's side of my family was there for me. My Mom's side of the family rid themselves of me. They thought it was the best thing to do at the time. Hey, my book would not have had this much drama without my crazy mother's crazy family and all the crazy things they did back in their day.

My Dad's side of the family was broken by what my Mom's side of the family decided for me. They are solid people though and they made decisions too. Maurice opened a Paternity Case to get me back. I was too afraid of what Drift and Eva would do to me if I let you win grandpa. They didn't just beat my body, but my mind as well. I am really feeling strong now that I know how much my Dad's side loved me. I love all of you too!

I wrote Chapter Eight for my friends and classmates. I am writing to you because some of you played a big part in helping me remember and verify my family. First of all, Thank You!

God Bless You All. Only children I knew revealed my story to me and tried to wake me up!

I would like to thank the ones who tried to tell me back so many years ago and to any of you who have shared the story about what you remember since. I know many of you remember my Dad. In Yet Another Town Wisconsin, my story was known in the Junior High and High School. I was in eighth grade. I knew high school students know because two of them wanted me in their band. How many high school seniors want to have an eighth grader in their band? NONE!

Unless the eighth grader could play music as easy as breathing and because my Dad Nevada Kidd was so well known? Do not take this the wrong way, I was flattered you asked and that we practiced a few times. I was a little afraid to play on stage at the high school. Please understand, it was hard to get a pass from any of the teachers for a high school event. Do you still play? I'm pretty sure I can get a pass now.

For now I would like to Thank Randolph in St. Something Town who wanted me to tell my Dad he could act and sing because you wanted to be in showbiz. God Bless You.

To Thank the bachelor in St Somewhere Town, he was a private eye. God Bless You.

A big Thank You to Rich Jackson and your friend in This Town on a Hill Wisconsin for wanting me in his band. God Bless You and your sister. Thanks for letting me drive again too. Nice Monte Carlo! That made me feel really good about myself. You are a prince.

Another big Thank You to Kitty in This Town on a Hill for telling Eva off, that was great. God Bless You.

Thank You to JJ in Yet Another Town. JJ even took me to meet her friends near Another Town I lived in who remembered me and tried to wake me up too!

This chapter is so I can keep a summary of what I just told you. I hope you enjoyed knowing a little more about me. I happen to think family is real important. I want to help others that have been adopted have hope. To have hope that even though our laws prevent most of us from meeting our families, it is possible to reconnect with them. I remember my family now after punishment to mind, soul and body. Even if I forget, I can read about it!

CHAPTER TEN

For My Future

Now for the future. I am ready for good and bad responses to my book. I only care about the good ones. I have had enough bad in my life so I tend to ignore it outright. If you think I cannot block the bad out, think again. It is the most important thing besides getting my memories back from Our Father in Heaven.

Most people instantly recognize Our Father in Heaven as God.

He is Our Father, which means he is everyone's creator and protector. Our Mother is the earth and our Mother protects us too. I have known Our Father and Our Mother since the beginning of time.

Our Father has never left my side. At first I thought there were cameras all around us. That is when I was younger. I remember how you protected me. You are a very Bright White Light. No one could misunderstand you when we are in your presence. Thank You for keeping me safe. Thank You for keeping me protected. Thank You for watching over me and my family.

There are good spirits involved.

Playing Our Father in Heaven forever and ever and he always will be himself, God.

We are his children and we are playing the roles of his sons and daughters forever.

Any one of us are playing the role as his prophets and it can be any one of us at any time.

I almost never knew any of this or my family without the help from Our Father in Heaven.

I will never forget any of you ever again.

I will never forget that Our Father in Heaven helped me and I know he always will.

I do not doubt my heritage on my Father's side of the family.

I wrote Chapter One for Our Father in Heaven and What I Remembered from Our Father.

I wrote Chapter Two for my son Arizona. I am writing down what was shown to me from above. I am writing down so that I never forget and so that no one else forgets either. Because of Arizona, I will always be able to stand up and protect him against evil people like the Walker's. Arizona will always play a big part in remembering our family.

I wrote Chapter Three for Arizona's family and his children to be born. I will be watching over them and when I cannot, Our Father in Heaven will watch them for me. It is not nice to show Our Father in Heaven how unhappy you are with one of his miracles. Thank him for them.

I wrote Chapter Four for the Unbelievers. Unbelievers like to do bad things and enjoy the bad rewards they receive. Otherwise they would change the way they make decisions.

I wrote Chapter Five for my real Parents, I love you and I always will, forever.

I wrote Chapter Six for my Brothers and Sisters. I love you, forever.

I wrote Chapter Seven for my Grandparents, Uncles and Aunts. I love all of you whether you love me or not. I know who wanted me back and hope that somehow my Grandfather will be forgiven for making a bad decision and putting me and others through hell. I am one strong son-of-a-bitch! When I put my shoulder down or my arm out, I get through what I have too.

I wrote Chapter Eight for my friends and Classmates. I hope none of you had to go through anything like this. If you did, I hope that you received and accepted help from Our Father. You can depend on him, believe me.

I always wanted to be a reporter and a messenger ever since I was born.

Signing off for now, Drift Walker, WAIT!

I'm Lucky McGillicudy Kidd now. Call me Lucky!

I'm making a good show and helping others now.

CHAPTER ELEVEN

Faith's Perspective, A Women's Perspective

His name is Drift 'Lucky' Walker. His nickname is Lucky, because that is what he is, Lucky.

We had to come up with fictitious names until official documentation is found or DNA is done. I am sure this will happen at some time or another. "Everything in its time" I seem to use clichés, because that's what I do. Glad Lucky finds it so cute. So we picked names that most describe the person who is being written about. Because of legal reasons and a required Content Evaluation, we have to say the names were changed to protect the innocent. Too many details could tip the reader off and easily identity someone who does not want to be identified.

I believe his story is true.

Most people who Lucky has told his story to over the many years have found it unbelievable. Lucky and I are polite mannerly people. We never dream of being vulgar or pushy. I was there when Lucky contacted his mom, getting to talk with her the day after Valentine's day. He was so happy, his mom said "I will help you" with emphasis on the will. I heard her. It was like she had been asked by others and she thought Lucky had validity. She declined getting together stating very poor health and no longer able to drive. She has not called back. Lucky has talked to her friend who answers her phone two times since. He states she is unwell and "just can't do this at this time because of her poor health".

Lucky reached out to his sister over social media. She was too little to remember him so she contacted me and asked about him. As I am writing this reply message to her a monster headache sets in. Here I am with the pressure building in my head all I wanted to do was close my eyes. Knowing how important this was and Lucky sitting right next to me wondering what I would say. I sent her back the message trying to convey information through a splitting headache, I hope it got through. Lucky was happy with what I sent. I had to apologize for not giving her more information. She never responded to my message. She never talked with Lucky at all. Well at least she thanked me in advance.

He often takes leaps of Faith now and he discovered I do also. Life has led me down this road.

It is awesome for me because by my very nature I am skeptical, slow to decide the truth. Trust has to be earned for me. My childhood friend Mary, got a dose of this when I questioned the very existence of God when we were young. I have since learned our Creator is very real. It was refreshing to talk with Lucky, he is always validating my spiritual beliefs. And knowing he has been in the white light validates my beliefs even more. I have yet to see it, thus my faith.

Lucky is here telling his story because he is so very lucky to be alive. When I met him April of 2013 we had common interests in natural healing and gardening. He was recovering from an injury most people never survive much less heal from with no repercussions. We started spending more time together each day finding out more about our spiritual connections. After a while he found out he could trust me. Not long before this my memory started becoming more solid. At first I thought it was because I studied the Tarot and Spirituality. Now I know it is because I am a witness. My memory has gone from regular memories like anyone else, you know like childhood and school and stuff to me paying far more attention to what happens.

I have a lot better recall for what happens in front of me.

I have discovered I am a catalyst. I am an empath. Introverted and quiet until I get comfortable. I am uncomfortable with long phone conversations. My family can vouch for that.

Lucky is extroverted, and looks forward to playing his drums and telling his story for others. His story hopefully will give faith to those that doubt the afterlife.

I always want to know what makes a person tick, why did they react the way they did because I am a detective at heart. My mom said "Your biggest fault is that you always see the good in a person, and it is also your greatest asset"

Lucky is a reporter at heart, a detective a scribe and a whole lot more. Every time I see someone misbehaving I try and come up with a reason why they behave that way. I know that life is hard here, if it were not hard we would be in Heaven. Another reason not to Judge. I have faith and having Lucky around gives me more support in having faith.

I have discovered some of us are Lighthouses and some of us are Sleepwalkers. I think it fits nicely that we ended up naming Lucky's foster parents The Walkers. I have discovered men can have really deep feelings about family. Maybe it is a Libra quality most men I have known did not care so much. Hope lives on in him, even after many disappointments and rejections. Lucky has survived incidents that kill people every day. He saw the white light more than once. He knows things and now he tries to make a good show, knowing God is recording every moment, every thought. Being honorable. He promised he would tell. God sent Lucky here and saved him from death so he could tell the story.

It is a story told many times down through history. The story of how mankind can make mistakes when society dictates the rules. The story of what happens to little children who are born to mothers who are too young according to society The story of how rich famous people are just like the regular people when it comes to society's rules. Lucky's real parents were in love when they made him, they told him so.

Thanks to the white light Lucky has memories of his past. I know he could not be the good person he is in his soul without any love involved. Lucky, what a perfect name for him. I hated calling him his other name, forced on him by someone not honorable.

Lucky asked me if I would give my perspective to the story. History. His story. I certainly have my own perspective, just as each and every reader has. Your soul resonates to the truth. I feel honored he would like to include me. He wanted his sisters input at first. We know she cares about animals on the social media sight. Sister Lady Slipper all your brother wants is to hug you and share stories about your Dad. Nothing else. I have never held back my opinions on Lucky. To me, it is, what it is. I doubt he would even change a word I write, unless it was to fix a typo. I would do the same for him.

IMAGINE, JOHN LENNON

Some of us are sleepwalkers, some of us are Lighthouses. There are moments in life when we get to choose which one we will be. We all have a place and purpose. You know when you are a lighthouse because you have discovered, "What goes around comes around". There I go again. You also believe the great teachers when they say, "Not to Judge". There is a reason not to judge. Everyone finds out exactly why when they are in the white light. We are all being recorded. Like Lucky says "Make a good show". Everyone finds out why not to Judge. Let's pray that elected Judges are really fair men for even they will see the white light when the time is right. Even good Judges can make the wrong decision.

Only shooting stars break the mold. Be in a good show. Everybody is different and that is okay. That is why we are here now. Our souls learn it is best not to judge, but to love. Honor the honorable. How you treat others, even animals, is your Karma. How they treat you is their Karma.

In my perspective Lucky's base story is how the little children should be protected. He was a highly sensitive little child. High energy also with his own sense of justice.

Bad choices like some neglect by a young mother who was still in high school. Both families were well known so hiding a love baby was even more difficult. Lucky was full of energy and raw emotion. His mother's father called him bad names and scared him. When he found out where his grandfather took him, to an orphanage, he refused to talk like he had been talking. He was very hurt and it made him angry and he said things out of hurt like many people do.

I have a lot of memories of childhood even before my memory got solid but he remembers more, always the same though. That's how I know he is not a liar. No one ever has to lie to me. I would not judge you, who am I to judge? You all get to judge your own actions with the white light when it is time. With gratitude I live each day. Thankful for reminding me we are here for you. To perfect our souls. I was born in an age and time where I learned not to Judge. The youngest female of the youngest female. All my relatives ready to pass over. Me left behind ready to comfort the living able to reassure them that we will see our loved ones again on the other side. Lucky calls me Yoda. I laugh and say Hmmm…..

If one little child can be spared any pain due to the word getting out because of this book it will have been worth the hard times. It will be worth the time it took to write it down and the struggle and frustration that comes with putting out a book and trying to make a living.

I have lived a blessed life. All the people I have learned from have helped me become the person I am today. Help those young ones. Take note when a little child says someone is hurting them. This is key. Take note.

The white light saved Lucky many times reinforcing his memory and his promise to tell this story, to share this story. Lucky has many stories to share, hopefully before very long we can share the actual names.

I told Lucky he was slapping the face of society. He told me he was punching society right in the face. Lucky is Karma.

Take note. Music brings people together.

More reasons to keep the faith.

Synchronicity turns me from being skeptical into jaw dropping, eye opening wide, goose bumpy grins from ear to ear awesome feeling inside. More validation.

Coincidence. When coincidence keeps happening it is no longer a coincidence.

Lucky being psychic. The way the Universe put us together. Timing of events like puzzle pieces or cogs that fit together just at the right time. Deja Vu. Dreams.

It was last summer when in my dream I saw Lucky and I, just our heads, slowly coming together, to kiss…and BLAM I was hit by lightning. I rose up in my bed, I was astonished at what just happened. We were and had been great friends until then. Well I did ask for spark. My feelings developed after that. Lucky is very patient with me, I'm hitting menopause. He has to be!

Music. The rhythm and timing.

Signs. The Eternity sign. The sideways racetrack.

Take note. Coincidence.

Lucky and I have many of the same tests in life. Patience is a tough one. It really feels better when you use it. Lucky uses it when appropriate and likes to make a good show. All I have ever seen Lucky do is good. We are both artists. I am watching and now I am more patient. I take life as it comes. To me the meaning of life is experience. Experience it. I hope I am not so dull as to not put on a good show.

As within, so without. As above, so below. All the great teachers have the same message. Space and time are not a factor. Your soul resonates to the truth. Listen to your heart. Follow your bliss. Lucky and I have a message and a mission. Everyone here does too.

You may have a question. You may have an answer. We don't know until the time comes.

I have discovered Lucky has no fear. His only weakness is that he hopes to unite his blood ties. He is not pushy. He has gingerly reached out to his family, each day goes by with no phone call from them. I tell him to try just one more time. Maybe your mom feels better? They were always nice to him on the phone, telling him it was okay to call back. Lucky has not called them back yet. He feels disappointed they have not called him.

Beauty is the reflection of the magic inside your soul.

My name is Faith Keeper

Because that is what I am. It took me 54 years to find that out.

Take note, the time is now. That is key.

I am going to try to make a good show. I wish the best for you to make yours.

Printed in the United States
By Bookmasters